In the Shadow of
JESSE JAMES

Stella Frances James, 1882–1971.

In the Shadow of
JESSE JAMES

by

Stella F. James

Edited by Milton F. Perry

8

Published by
The Revolver Press
A Division of Dragon Books

Copyright © 1989 by Dragon Books
All Rights Reserved
ISBN No. 0 946062 29 3
Library of Congress Catalog Card No. 89-81371
First Published May 1990

Publisher David A. Chambers
Editor Milton F. Perry
Designer Nancy Haberman
Illustration Wendy Wees
Calligraphy Shirley Frankel

For Ethelrose

Thou are not one of the living now;
    And yet a form appears
At times before me, such as thou
    In Days of former years:
It rises, to my spirit's sight,
In thoughts by day, in dreams at night.

Nor can I choose, but fondly bless
    A shade, if shade it be,
Which, with such soft expressiveness
    Recalls one thought of thee:
I own it, in itself, ideal;
Its influence o'er my heart is real.

I grant these dreams are idle things,
    Yet I have known a few,
To which my faithful memory clings;
    They seem'd so sweet and true,
That, let who will the fault condemn,
It was a grief to wake from them.

Bernard Barton

Acknowledgements

The Publisher wishes to take this opportunity to thank all those who contributed to the production of this book. Special thanks go to our editor, Milton F. Perry, whose dedication to his profession has won the admiration of us all.

———— •·•— ————

Errors, like straws, upon the surface flow,
He who would search for pearls must dive below.

———— •·•— ————

CONTENTS

Jesse James in 1875. It is believed this photograph, taken in Nebraska City, Nebraska, was the last picture taken of him while he was alive. This is how he appeared when he married Zerelda Mimms a year earlier. Courtesy Ethelrose James.

PREFACE

I shall not write on the history of Frank and Jesse James as hunted men or outlaws. The legend of Jesse James has already been given to four generations, via the ten-cent novel and stark melodrama of the most lurid sort.

I do not claim to personally know the truth about the father of the man I married. I was just five weeks old when he was killed in St. Joseph, Missouri on April 3rd, 1882. I can tell, however, the things I have learned about the famous badman from the people who knew him, and did not believe that Jesse was bad by nature. I know what the people who were closest to him, his wife, his mother and his brother had to say about the famous outlaw. As the wife of Jesse James, Jr., for more than fifty years, I came to know the James family very well.

Zerelda Samuel, the mother of Jesse and Frank James, spent two winters in our home. Frank James and his wife, Anna, visited our home many times, and we visited them in their home on the James farm. John Samuel, the half brother of Jesse, was very close to Jesse, Jr., and his family.

Sallie Samuel Nicholson and Fannie Samuel Hall, half-sisters to Jesse and Frank lived on farms near the old James home in Kearney, Missouri, which was only thirty miles from our home in Kansas City. Jesse, Jr., and I enjoyed taking our four daughters to visit these farm homes where there was an abundance of friendliness and hospitality. These people were quiet, industrious farmers, highly respected by the community and liked by their neighbors.

Three members of the James family had been closest to Jesse James; of all the world, they knew best the truth about his life. They all talked often and freely to Jesse, Jr. and me about the boyhood and youth of Jesse James; about his years as a hunted outlaw, about the hopes and dreams he had cherished in the face of insurmountable adversity, about the efforts and plans he had made to give his wife and his two children a better future—plans which were doomed by his murder, when his son was but six years old.

My purpose in writing this books is twofold. First, I want to answer some of the questions that have been asked of us in the hundreds of letters we have received. Secondly, I want to expose a few of the many the imposters, who have claimed to be Jesse James come back to life.

The last of them, John James and Frank Dalton with whom I had personal contact, only because they chose to annoy my sick husband and other members of my family. I will also deal with yet another imposter who claims to be Jesse James the Third, which of course is impossible, as we did not have a son.

This, then, is my account of a part of the Legend. And this account is true.

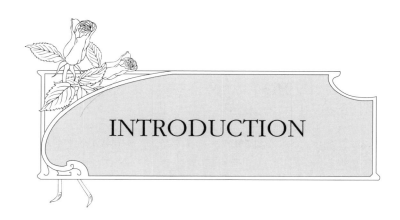

INTRODUCTION

I n April, 1958, Stella James, widow of Jesse James, Jr., and her family saw the preview of "Bitter Harvest," a production of the television series "Playhouse 90." Her husband was portrayed as a gunfighter and it incensed her. The picture has been long forgotten but we should be grateful to the producers for her reaction.

"This was a great shock to me and my family," she wrote another Missourian, Harry S. Truman, September 27th, 1961, "and as I did not have a horse, never owned a gun and traffic was too heavy to ride to the studio anyway, I decided to write a book."

This is that book.

Neither Jesse nor Frank James ever wrote their memoirs, nor did any member of their family. Jesse, as we all know, was slain by "that dirty little coward" of ballad infamy on April 3rd, 1882; Frank lived to be seventy-two, but never published any accounts of his years as an outlaw—indeed he had sufficient reason: though he had been acquitted of implication in a train robbery and murder, and a payroll holdup, there were at least a dozen such incidents he could have been charged with if he had admitted participation.

Zee, Jesse's widow, signed a contract with a publisher soon after her husband's death and gave at least one interview, but soon withdrew. She also tried stage appearances but they were so poorly received they were cancelled after the second one. Though she lived in dire poverty for twenty

Stella Frances James with daughters Lucille and Josephine.
Circa 1904.

years, raised two children and died very poor, she refused many offers from publishers.

Frank's widow, Anna, outlived him by nearly thirty years. She too, steadfastly refused to be interviewed and never wrote her reminiscences, and, when visitors arrived for tours of the James Farm given by her son and his wife, she would retreat into the south parlor and close the door.

Zerelda Samuel, the formidable mother of the James Boys, loved to tell her stories to reporters and "curiosity seekers" at the Farm, but never discussed her son's careers of outlawry. That, she would claim, was "a military secret."

And what stories they could have told! What really happened at Northfield? Who killed the teller? Who was at the Liberty and Gallatin robberies and who shot "Jolly" Wymore and Captain Sheets? Did Frank and Jesse know that conductor Westfall of the train stopped at Winston had been the conductor of the train that took the detectives to Kearney when they attacked their mother's home and killed their young half-brother and maimed her? Who fired back from the cabin that horrible night and wounded one of the detectives? Did they or the detectives kill their neighbor Dan Askew? Who shot the detective Whicher? And how much money did their robberies really produce?

Alas, we will never know!

Jesse, Jr. published a little book in 1899, *Jesse James My Father*. However, it only presents his father as seen through the eyes of a seven-year-old. We do not see Jesse, the bandit. In 1903, two books by gang members Cole Younger and Jim Cummins added little. They had the same reasons as Frank James for their reticence.

This is why Stella's book is important: it is the only account written by another family member, an "insider." She knew and writes about Zee James, Zerelda Samuel, Frank and Anna James, Sallie Nicholson, Perry Samuel, Reuben Samuel, Mary James and of course, Jesse, Jr. They all knew Jesse James, and her accounts of what they told her give us details and bits and pieces of what it was like to have been with him. But further, she also tells us what his widow and their children and their children's children had to endure, and the calumnies that went with the name. But times change. Today those same persons would be sought after for autographs and the posing of photographs.

Stella Frances McGown was a beautiful seventeen-year-old country girl when she attended the dance where she met the man she would marry. Sweet, charming and unsophisticated, she proved to be made of strong stuff, and for the last twenty-five years of her marriage was the mainstay of her family. Possessed of less than a high school education, she wrote a book as charming and interesting as she was.

Though she knew every intimate detail of family quarrels, likes and dislikes, she chose to overlook them and speaks only the best of everyone. Her task was not to open closets, but to let us see the people—and of course Jesse James—through her eyes. Passions ran high among the relatives but not in Stella's book. If she shared them, she does not tell us. And it is well she didn't, for it allows us to keep our eyes on the true focal figure: Jesse.

The book was, for her, a way of getting justice for her family. While researching for this book I was most struck by the similarity of the reasons Stella and Zee Mimms both gave for accepting their Jesse Jameses in marriage. Both of these men had been charged with train robbery and it took a great deal of character for these girls to marry them. At least, Stella had the support of her family; Zee never saw her mother again. Not to be outshone is the elopement of Anna Ralston, the lovely school teacher daughter of one of Independence, Missouri's best families, with the outlaw Frank James. All three women were pretty, bright and intelligent, and all three found reasons for accepting these husbands. None was ever quoted as regretting their choice.

My research, for the first time, presents documented details of a number of events. The exciting wedding of Jesse and Zee, their honeymoon, and the incredible residence in

Kansas City in the summer of 1881 with its successful, as well as aborted train robberies, and Jesse's almost normal way of life there, living next to the family of the County Marshal! I found details about the elopement of Anna and Frank, an exciting romance. I am also able to present a study of the almost invisible Dr. Reuben Samuel, the boys beloved stepfather, and Zerelda James' strange second marriage and how it created a distant relationship between the Jameses, Youngers, Daltons and Johnny Ringo.

Stella's stories, supported by the researched appendices, cast new light onto niches of the epic saga of one of the best known Americans.

Hers is a charming, witty, yet sad book, written in her own beautiful distinctive style. I have not changed it or her arrangement of the chapters. I have identified people as she meets them and have checked dates and spellings, and searched and found articles she quoted. My other contribution has been to add explanatory footnotes and appendices to reveal more of the story behind the story, that of Jesse James.

It is above all else, Stella's book.

I owe debts of gratitude to Ethel Rose Owens, Stella's surviving daughter, who answered my questions and sent me interesting bits of material; David Chambers, our pleasant and erudite publisher, and, of course, my wife Janet, who "lost" her husband to Stella many evenings and weekends.

&. Milton F. Perry
Director of Historical Research and Development
Clay County, Missouri

I MEET
JESSE JAMES

He may not have been the most handsome man at the Valentine's party,[1] though certainly I thought he was at the time. (And I never afterward had any cause to think otherwise.)

But there was never any way to be sure that he was the handsomest, and the most gallant, as well as the most attentive, because he scarcely gave me any chance to look around at the others who were there so I might compare.

Not that I would have done much looking around at the men in any case. At least, not in any obvious way. Nice girls just didn't, in those days. Do they now? Manners change, in the course of half a century or so. Even the nicest girls are a good deal more candid, more spontaneous now, it seems to me.

But I can't imagine any girl, now any more than then, wanting to show as much concern about the whole problem of men as I actually felt that night, when I first arrived at that party.

I didn't even have an escort, not a man of my own. Just Sam, the brother of my older sister's beau, who had goodnaturedly agreed to round out the foursome so that I could tag along.

I was young, only seventeen. And we were fairly new in town. Our family had moved to Kansas City from our old

---

[1]February, 1899

farm near Ash Grove, in the southern part of Missouri, where I had spent my childhood. I hadn't been to very many parties in my whole life so far, and never before to any in the "big city."

Now here I was, in my prettiest blue silk with white lace on the sleeves, my hair piled high in a fashion to which I was not yet accustomed, feeling both frightened and thrilled and wishing I could really be part of it with a beau of my own, instead of just included because I was somebody's kid sister.

Other boys and girls, some around my age, most a bit older, were milling around beneath the streamers of red and white bunting and big red paper hearts which made up the Valentine decorations. Everybody seemed to be laughing, calling to each other, waving the sealed white envelopes we had all been handed as we entered.

Then suddenly a very tall, strikingly handsome young man was standing before me. "Do you think you could be my partner?" he asked.

I couldn't answer. I could only look up at him in astonishment.

He was smiling, but his blue eyes were grave. His question had been perfectly serious, I realized. But I didn't know what to say.

Just then our hostess, who must have observed my dilemma, came to my rescue.

"Have you two met?" she asked pointedly. After all, it was simply not correct for a young man to approach a young lady until he had been properly introduced.

When I said, "No", she said, "Stella McGown, may I present Jesse James!"

At this I had to laugh. She had certainly put him in his place! Everyone knew Jesse James had been a daring outlaw, and the name well-suited this bold young man.

He laughed, too, and thanked our hostess for the

introduction, adding, "I have found a partner."
She was quick to correct him. For our supper partners,
we were supposed to match the half of the torn valentine
that was in our sealed envelope. The young man obligingly
displayed his torn valentine, and smiled again.

I had not yet opened my envelope, and I did so now
with fingers that insisted on trembling. When I produced
my half of the valentine, it matched his perfectly! This was
the beginning of our romance.

Everything in my whole young world seemed to fall in
place at that moment. Everything about this handsome
young stranger seemed to match my girlish hopes and
dreams perfectly.

Shyness was quickly forgotten. We had so much to talk
about, all of a sudden, there might just as well not have been
anybody else at the party, for all we noticed or cared.

The evening was half over before I thought to ask him
his real name.

"Jesse James is my real name," he replied. "Jesse
James, *Jr.*"[2]

[2]Although he was generally referred to as "Jesse James, Jr" his actual
name was Jesse Edwards James. Born in Nashville, Tennessee on
August 31st 1875, he was given this middle name in honor of John
Newman Edwards, founder and first editor of the *Kansas City Times*.
John Edwards had been a staunch friend and defender of both Jesse
and Frank James.

Jesse James, Jr., *Jesse James My Father* (Sentinel Press, Independence,
Mo. 1899), Page 5. Hereafter referred to in this text as *Jesse James, Jr.*
William A. Settle, Jr., *Jesse James Was His Name* (University of
Nebraska Press, Lincoln, Nebraska 1977), Page 129. Hereafter *Settle.*
Robertus Love, *The Rise and Fall of Jesse James* (G.P.Putnam & Sons,
New York 1926), Page 278. Hereafter *Love.*

Mrs. Jesse James, Jesse, Jr., and Mary. This sad photograph was taken in Kansas City on April 15, 1882, only two weeks after Jesse was shot, and shows the marks of grieving on her face. Courtesy Ethelrose James.

CHAPTER 2
TROUBLED CHILDHOOD

I t wasn't easy for me to win the consent of my parents for me to have a date with Jesse James, Jr. My parents set some store by family background. We took pride in the fact that we claimed, as part of my father's ancestry, no less distinguished a forebear than Daniel Boone.

My great-grandmother, Mary Boone Hosman, was the daughter of Nathan Boone and granddaughter of Daniel. She still lived on the old Nathan Boone Homestead near Ash Grove, Missouri.

Now, when I invited my new beau, Jesse, to my home to have my parents meet him, the atmosphere was somewhat strained. My mother and father were too courteous, and too kind, to show any outright hostility to this fine looking, pleasant mannered young man who came courting their daughter. But certainly they were not able to feel any enthusiastic approval toward the son of the notorious "Bad Man".

The Sunday afternoon of Jesse's third visit to my home, I could not help noticing how stiffly everyone seemed to be perched on the edge of the uncomfortable parlor chairs, how the conversation seemed to sputter nervously and die, how my younger brothers and sisters sat around and stared in excited curiosity at our guest.

My father (Alfred M. McGown) asked, "You say you live with your mother here in town, Mr. James?"

"Yes, sir, Mr. McGown," Jesse replied. "With my mother and sister, Mary."

I was wishing that he'd go on to explain that he'd bought and paid for their cottage himself out of his own earnings, for he'd been working hard to support the three of them ever since earliest boyhood. I wanted Jesse to make my parents see what a fine person he was.

But then my mother, (Martha) just trying to keep the faltering conversation going, and certainly not intending to be unkind, began, "And your father?" breaking off in dismay after realizing the blunder too late.

"He was killed, ma'am, back in 1882," said Jesse.[3] And a tense silence fell in the room, while my brothers and sisters[4] exchanged thrilled glances, and waited to see where this tantalizing turn of conversation might lead.

It led nowhere, for Jesse rose at this point and said to my father. "It's such a fine day, sir, I wonder if I might have your permission to take Stella for a buggy ride?"

I jumped up in relief as my father nodded his consent.

After Jesse had helped me into his buggy and started off down the street, I said, "I'm sorry Jesse. I'm sure Mother didn't mean anything by her question about your father."

"I'm sure she didn't", Jesse agreed quickly." And I would gladly have told her more about him. I will, someday, when she and your father no longer feel nervous about it."

"Well, *I* don't feel nervous about it," I said, quite truthfully. For, beyond the fact that the name James was considered practically synonymous with boldness and daring, I really knew very little about the famous—or infamous—"James Legend".

Jesse laughed. "Well then, I guess I can tell you now!" he said. He headed the horses out toward Woodland Ave-

[3]Jesse James was shot and killed in his St. Joseph, Missouri home on April 3rd, 1882 by Robert Ford.

[4] Stella Frances McGown, our author, was the second child born to Alfred M. and Martha McGown of a family of five girls and two boys.

nue and drove by the house where he'd lived with his parents and sister years ago, before they'd all moved to St. Joseph, Missouri.

"My folks called themselves 'Mr. and Mrs. Howard' in those days," Jesse said." And that was the only name that I knew for a long time."[5]

He pointed out a neighboring house and told me that a little boy had lived there, about his own age, and he'd wanted to play with him.

"But my mother said that we'd be leaving soon, and I would find another little boy to play with then. My father always painted a bright future for me, of going to school, meeting other children, riding horses on a farm. I didn't know at the time that there was any reason why the future might not work out just that way".

On the other side of the Woodland Avenue house, he went on, lived a Mr. Con Murphy, who was County Marshal and very anxious to find the James boys. Just back of Mr. Murphy's house was a vacant lot where a posse gathered on horseback. They would ride out near Independence and the "Cracker Neck District" to search for the James gang.

"One day," Jesse said, "my father went over to talk to Mr. Murphy and he wished him luck in his hunt for the James boys. Some time later my father packed us all up, and moved the family to St. Joe.[6] Remember, I was just a child, barely six years old. I still thought my name was Howard, until after my father was killed in St. Joe."

I had not yet met Jesse's mother. I knew she was quite ill. Now Jesse told me she had never been really well since

---

[5]Jesse James used the alias "J.T. Jackson" in Kansas City. In St. Joseph and Tennessee he was "Thomas Howard", while his wife was known as "Josie" and their son "Tim". *Kansas City Journal*, April 5th, 1882.

[6]Please see appendix.

her husband's death. Jesse and his sister had still been very small when their father was killed. It must have been a heavy burden for the young widow to go on and care for them alone.

"Lots of people thought my father left us rich," Jesse said. "But nothing could be further from the truth. Mother, Mary and I had practically nothing but the clothes on our backs after my father was gone.[7] We had a terrible struggle just trying to keep going, and I don't know what might have become of us if my Uncle Tom Mimms,[8] Mother's unmarried brother, hadn't taken us in. Because Mother insisted, and because I knew it was what my father would have wanted, I went ahead and finished three years of high school. Then I quit, and went to work instead."

Jesse had been twelve years old when he applied for, and got, a job as an office boy for the real estate firm of Thomas T. Crittenden, Jr. who happened to be the son of Thomas T. Crittenden, Governor of Missouri at the time Jesse James was killed. He held this job during school vacation for the next six years.

"I was too young to realize it at the time," Jesse told me." But in later years I could appreciate the irony of it: the son of Jesse James going to work for the son of Governor Crittenden, who had offered a reward for my father. I can assure you, however, that after I was hired for the job nothing was ever done to remind me of the unusual relation-

---

[7]When Jesse James was killed he left his family little money. His wife found it necessary to auction many of her household items. Please see appendix.

[8]Thomas M. Mimms and Zerelda James were among the twelve children of Mary James Mimms, older sister of Robert S. James, Jesse's father, and John Mimms. He worked for sixty years at the T.M. James China Co. which was owned by the uncle after whom he was named.

Jesse, Jr. as a youth. Courtesy Ethelrose James.

ship between the Crittendens and Jameses."

Jesse had been only one of many young boys to apply for that job. Tom Crittenden singled him out as the brightest and most promising of the group interviewed, and only then learned Jesse's identity.

Greatly surprised, Tom Crittenden nevertheless told him, "Well, Jesse, if your Mother and your Grandmother are willing for you to work for me, I will employ you."

He had been aware that Jesse's grandmother, Mrs. Zerelda Samuel, was very bitter against all state officials and officers, having had a hand blown off, and her little son, Archie, killed by Pinkerton detectives when they were searching for Jesse and Frank.[9]

"The next day," Jesse told me, "I went back to Tom Crittenden and told him I had the consent of my Mother and Grandmother to go to work for him. The job turned out fine, gave me a lot of experiences and some wonderful friendships. I stayed with it several years, until I was old enough to try another field. Then I got a position with Armour Packing Co. as a timekeeper, and worked there for six and a half years".[10] Jesse was athletic, I learned. It was at Armour Packing Co. that he'd started playing baseball on the company team. Now that he was in business for himself, he still played baseball with several other teams. On one of these, Johny Kling and Joe Tinker, later to become baseball greats, were teammates. He also played basketball with the Kansas

---

[9] January 25th, 1875.

[10] Jesse James, Jr. had worked part-time at the "Bee Hive" Department Store in downtown Kansas City when he was eleven; then for Crittenden and Phister Real Estate Company; The Germania Life Insurance Company; and Armour Packing Co. from June 21st, 1891, until January 15th, 1898. With the help of his friend Crittenden, he later ran a cigar stand in the lobby of the Jackson County Courthouse, and it was at this time that he met Stella. *Kansas City Journal*, Feb. 28, 1898.

City Athletic Club.

Jesse's first business venture was a cigar and tobacco counter which he opened in the County Court House of Kansas City, Missouri. He later opened a much larger store at 121 West 9th Street in Kansas City, across from the Orpheum Theatre. This was not what he really wanted to do with his life, he confided. His ambition was to go ahead and complete his education, study law and become an attorney.

"You'll do it, too, Jesse," I told him, as we drove that Sunday afternoon. "I have faith in you to accomplish just about anything you set out to do!"

"Do you really?" he asked, as the buggy pulled up in front of my house. "Well, then, you can expect to start wearing a ring on this finger very soon". He clasped my left hand tenderly, and added: "And maybe you'd better start getting used to the name, James."

I blushed, but I didn't protest, because I knew he was right. In fact, though I would never admit it, I had already started "practicing" the name to myself, so sure was I that he would propose sooner or later.

But I hadn't expected it this soon. And I couldn't help wondering a bit, how long it would take my family to accept the name, James.

Jesse, Jr. circa 1900. Courtesy Ethelrose James

CHAPTER 3

FIGHT FOR JUSTICE

My parents knew that I was falling in love with Jesse. And they, too, were beginning to like and respect him.

How could they help it? At the age of twenty-two, he was already a self-made man in the finest American tradition.

He had come a long way since his first job as an office boy. Having worked and help support his family since the age of eleven, he had bought their modest home and put his sister Mary through school. [11] By the time I met him, Jesse had an enviable reputation among men of prominence here in Kansas City as a substantial young businessman with a promising future.

One would think that he had lived down the past and completely cleared his family's name of the old notoriety. But such was not the case.

It seemed that less than a year before, a vicious attempt had been made to revive the sensationalism of the James past and to convict young Jesse of a crime of violence, a recent train robbery, of which he was completely innocent.

---

[11]"He (T.T. Crittenden, Jr.) sold to my mother the lot of ground in Kansas City and loaned us the money to build a modest house on it, taking my notes for the amount and assuring us that the notes should *(sic)* never go out of his hands, and that we should *(sic)* have our own time in which to pay them off. He kept his word." *Jesse James, Jr.* 116-117.

This was 1898. There had been a daring train robbery near Kansas City. The newspapers called it "A perfect pattern of a Jesse James robbery".[12] Jesse, Jr., who had never committed any crime in all his young life, except to be born the son of an outlaw, was promptly arrested and brought to trial for this robbery!

It was a warm spring evening, with the trees around my house beginning to show lacy trimmings of green buds and the sky in the west holding the sunset glow until well past supper, when Jesse sat down on the veranda with my parents to tell us the truth about this tragic episode in his life and try to put our minds at ease about it.

It was strange to me, in such a peaceful, pleasant setting, to listen to this story of such a shocking outrage perpetrated on the most decent and honorable young man I had ever known.

"Believe me," Jesse told us, gravely, "I learned what it means to have friends, real friends. Without the moral and material help these friends gave me, the detectives' conspiracy to ruin me might have succeeded. Former Governor Crittenden[13] was one of the first to come to my support. He declared openly that he believed I was innocent. His son, Tom, Jr., was another friend who stood by me through thick and thin."

The golden shimmer in the west was fading and night shadows gathered. Soon the veranda on which we sat was plunged in darkness and we could no longer see Jesse's face. But the trembling tone of his deep voice revealed the emotion he felt as he described Tom Crittenden's visit to him immediately after his arrest for robbery.

---

[12] Please see appendix

[13] Who had offered the reward for which the elder Jesse was killed in 1882.

"Tom said to me, 'Jesse I've known you since you were a little boy. I've watched you and admired you and had complete faith in you since the day you came to work for me. Now I want you to tell me the plain truth and the whole truth about this train robbery. I want you to tell me if you had anything to do with it or know anything about it.'

"I answered him, 'Tom, you are as good a friend as I have on earth. No one ever knew a James to go back on a friend. If I'd lie to you now I ought to be hanged like a dog. I tell you I am absolutely innocent, and all I ask is a fair trial and I'll prove it.'

"He said, 'I'm going to accept your statement of innocence. I believe you are telling me the truth and I'm going to stand by you.'"

At that time, Jesse told us, Crittenden was a candidate for re-election to the office of Clerk of Jackson County, Missouri. He was staking his political career on Jesse's innocence. Soon many others pledged themselves to the fight, out of friendship for Jesse and devotion to Justice. Through their combined efforts they succeeded in obtaining a fair trial, with Judge Dorsey W. Shackleford presiding. The jury acquitted Jesse on the first ballot.

"I vowed then," Jesse said, "that through no fault of my own shall these men ever have cause to regret that they gave me the hand of friendship. I intend to go right on with the course I set for myself long ago, to prove myself as a businessman and a citizen and worthy of the respect of the public and friendship of those who choose to be my friends."

I felt a great lump in my throat as I sat down there in the darkness, and I knew my parents were deeply stirred, too.

Presently my mother sighed. "But you must feel bitter toward those awful men who tried to ruin your life," she said, sympathetically.

Jesse thought for a moment before replying, "I can

honestly say I bear no ill will toward anyone. You see, some of my best friends are men who were Federal soldiers who fought my father and were fought by him in honorable warfare. I'm sure that if my father were living today, he would be a friend to these former enemies, too. I don't believe in grudges, or revenge. I believe in letting bygones be bygones and forgetting old grievances. I remember that in Lexington, at the close of the war, my father and the man that shot and almost killed him, afterwards became close personal friends.[14] One thing I have learned: there is good in every man."

"Strikes me," my father said, "You've inherited the best of the good that was in your father, Jesse. I'm very glad to hear you talk that way about him."

"Thank you, sir," Jesse said. He sounded a little embarrassed by my father's unexpected warmth.

I imagine Jesse was probably thankful for the darkness which cloaked the emotions he was experiencing; and so was I, for I knew that my normally gruff, matter-of-fact father would never have permitted himself such an expression of sentiment had it not been for the comfort of the shadows of the balmy spring night.

After a while, my mother suggested that we all come into the kitchen for some lemonade and cookies. It was cozy in there and the light was bright. In the next room my brothers and sisters were noisy and cheerful over a lively game of dominoes. The solemn mood that had engulfed us on the veranda quickly vanished. Soon Jesse, my parents and I were laughing and talking about quite ordinary things.

It was only later, after we all said good night and I had gone to my own room to go to bed, that the earlier mood

---

[14] Jesse James was shot near Lexington, Missouri, on May 15th 1865, in a skirmish with Union soldiers. Please see appendix.

returned as I unfolded the newspaper clipping Jesse had given me to read.

It was from the *Kansas City World* of May 21st, 1899:

"The friendship existing between Tom Crittenden, County Clerk, and Jesse James, Jr., is quite well known in Kansas City. The newspapers referred to it often during the recent trial of the boy on a charge of train robbery, and many marveled at evidences of a fellowship so staunch as to outlive the effects of the evil report against this scion of Jesse James, Sr., the bandit. Mr. Crittenden never doubted the innocence of his protege. Though the trial occurred in the heat of a political campaign, in which Mr. Crittenden was a candidate for re-election, and when to avow sympathy for an accused train robber was to make enemies, still he stood by young James, and helped him with his time, money and influence.

A political campaign was on. Crittenden was a candidate on the Democratic ticket for re-election. The campaign was a warm one and the question of train robbery was an issue in it.

Under those circumstances and in the face of that sort of campaign, it was perilous for a Democratic candidate to openly avow his championship for one of the alleged train robbers. But Crittenden made no halfway business of it.

He furnished the bond for Jesse's release. He retained lawyers to defend him and helped gather evidence to acquit him. He was criticized severely for this, and it was even said that his action would cause the defeat of all Democratic candidates. Then came the acquittal of Jesse, but not before the day of the election brought the re-election of Crittenden.

"After the acquittal, Crittenden assisted Jesse in renting and stocking a cigar store in one of the principal streets, and the young man attends strictly to business and is making money. His best friend yet is T.T. Crittenden, Jr."

After I had read it through twice, I folded the clipping, put it away, and sat on the bed for a long time, brushing my hair and thinking.

If I really intended to marry Jesse, I would have to worry about this kind of thing happening again. And I would have to worry about "what people might say."

But then I recalled how Jesse himself had described the whole sordid episode to us, straightforwardly, without a trace of self pity or malice toward his enemies. No matter what might happen to that young man, I knew that nothing would ever break that fine spirit or daunt that noble heart.

And what about the way people might talk? After what had been said in Jesse's praise by some of the most prominent men in Missouri and by a fearless and forthright newspaper like the *Kansas City World*, why should I ever worry about what others might say?

I would be proud, I decided, to be the wife of a man whose strength of character had proven equal to the challenge.

After I put out the light, before going to sleep in the quiet solitude of my own bed, I whispered it out loud: "I would be *proud* to be called Mrs. Jesse James."

CHAPTER 4

MY FUTURE HOME

O n my first visit to Jesse's house, I was almost too overcome with shyness and excitement to take in my surroundings.

I was getting my first glimpse, after all, of the home which would be mine after I married Jesse. But all I noticed was that it was a pleasant little cottage, furnished with more simplicity (and I thought more charm) than was fashionable in that period of ornate and Rococo decoration.[15]

That day, because the summer weather was fair, the rooms were filled with sunshine. In contrast to my own home, which usually resounded with the sound of healthy, growing children this house seemed unnaturally hushed and still.

The reason for the quiet became apparent when Jesse led me into the small sitting room, where heavy curtains were drawn against the sunlight, and introduced me to his mother.

Zee James[16] looked very small and fragile, propped on

[15] Zee's house stood originally at 3402 Tracy Avenue, Kansas City. Long thought to have been torn down, it was recently discovered at 1211 East 34th Street to where it had been moved. It has changed very little in appearance. Please see appendix.

[16] Zerelda Amanda Mimms James was born July 21st, 1845. She was named for Zerelda Cole James, the mother of the man she would marry. Her mother, Mary, was a sister of the Rev. Robert S. James, the father of Jesse and Frank.

Mrs. James seated on the porch of her home at 3402 Tracy Avenue, Kansas City, Missouri. Courtesy Ethelrose James.

many pillows in an armchair that seemed much too large for her, with a woolen blanket covering her knees despite the warmth of the day, and a white woolen shawl around her thin shoulders.

Her gentle face was almost as white as the shawl, and I could see for myself that she was as ill as Jesse told me she was. He had told me that his mother had never really been well since his father's death, and he had also said that his own arrest the year before for train robbery had shattered what little health his mother still had, leaving Jesse and his sister in despair over her condition.

But if Zee James was broken in health and spirit, she still retained the gracious inclinations of a gentle heart.

Motioning me to a chair near her own, she said, "Please sit down, my child. I hope you can forgive an old lady for not having arranged some suitable entertainment for your first visit to our home. You see, I haven't been well."

I was astonished that she should feel there was any need to apologize, and, in some confusion, tried to say so.

But Jesse and his mother both had the ability to put people at their ease, and soon the three of us were conversing pleasantly about all sorts of things, including our wedding plans.

"I do wish I could attend," Mrs. James sighed, her first and only expression of despondency over her illness.

"But you will, Mother," Jesse assured her warmly. "Stella and I both insist that you be present at our wedding. We wouldn't have it any other way!"

Zee James smiled sadly and shook her head. Her blue eyes turned to me. "What date have you set?" she asked.

I replied that we were planning to be married a year hence in June.

"June." Mrs. James repeated. "A lovely month for a wedding."

Presently we were joined by Jesse's sister, Mary, a very attractive young woman several years older than myself whose wit and poise I greatly admired[17] Suggesting that it was time she tucked her mother into bed for her rest, Mary bustled about briskly and cheerfully, attending to the many little chores she obviously was in the habit of doing for Mrs. James' comfort.

I said my good-byes and thank-you, hoping that our visit had not tired the old lady unduly, and Jesse and I went out to wander about the little garden in the bright sunlight for a while.

When Mary rejoined us there, she said to me, "Mother so much enjoyed meeting you, Stella. She likes you very much. We're both happy that Jesse is making you one of the family."

Then she turned to Jesse and said, "I know that you and Stella have made your plans, and neither Mother nor I would

---

[17] Mary Susan James was born June 17th, 1879 in Tennessee. She was three years old when her father was killed. Please see appendix.

Zerelda Mimms James, wife and first cousin of Jesse Woodson James, and called by him "Zee." Courtesy Ethelrose James.

want you to change them in any way. But perhaps you would want to think about the possibility that we may be able to take Mother to Hot Springs by the time the cold weather sets in".

I glanced at Jesse, wondering what this might mean. A young bride-to-be never likes the possibility of being separated from her intended, no matter how urgent the reason for the separation might be.

Jesse explained that he and Mary had been hoping their mother would be well enough by winter, to make the trip to Hot Springs, Arkansas, where they believed her condition might be helped.

"Of course", I said, "you must do what is best for your mother. And if this should cause a change in our plans ... "

Jesse smiled into my eyes to show me he knew he could count on me to agree to whatever might be necessary.

After we'd chatted a while longer in the pleasant garden with Mary, we turned to leave.

I cast a last wistful glance at the cottage, as Jesse helped me into the buggy. It looked so peaceful, basking in the slanted rays of the late afternoon sun. Someday it would be my home.

CHAPTER 5

A WINTER WEDDING

Our wedding plans were changed, all right. But not in the way I'd expected—and feared. I had assured Jesse I would agree to any change that might be necessary. And I had meant it. So I certainly did not protest when it was decided, quite suddenly, that instead of being married in June, we would move the date up to January!

So it was that less than a year after I first met him, I became the wife of Jesse James, Jr.

Zee James had become too ill to go to Hot Springs, or even to attend her son's wedding.

Jesse did what he could to bring the wedding to her, by taking the entire wedding party in two horse-drawn, unheated cabs, all the way across town in near-zero weather, to stand by her bedside as we had stood at the wedding, so that she might see how we looked during the ceremony. We were married by Reverend S.H. Werlein of the Methodist Church, who was Zee James' minister.[18] Among the guests at our wedding, there were two whose personalities stood out from the rest so vividly that I later found myself remem-

---

[18] Stella and Jesse Jr., were married in the parlor of her parents' home at 415 Landis Court, Kansas City, at 8 p.m. on January 24th, 1900. The ceremony was performed by Rev. Dr. S.H. Werlein of the Kansas City Methodist Church, South. Please see appendix.

Jesse, Jr. and Stella on their wedding day. Courtesy Ethelrose James.

bering them often. One was Elizabeth West,[19] who was called "Aunt Liz West" by the James family. She was Jesse's great aunt and sister of the first Jesse's father, the Reverend Robert S. James. Aunt Elizabeth was a true aristocrat. At our wedding, she looked like she had stepped out of a painting, in her lavender taffeta and cream lace.

In contrast was my grandmother, Mary F. Prunty[20], my

[19] Elizabeth James, a sister of the father of Frank and Jesse, married Tillman Howard West in Kentucky, and moved to Missouri in 1844. Among his businesses was a large men's clothing store in Kansas City. He and Elizabeth helped organize the Methodist Episcopal Church, South, there. He died on October 3rd, 1884 and she on December 2nd, 1904.

[20] Mary F. Prunty, (1842-1932) was the eldest daughter of Mary Boone and Alfred Hosman and a granddaughter of Nathan, son of Daniel Boone. Her marriage to Dr. Robert Cole Prunty on March 22nd, 1863 was her second, she being the widow McGown. The child of her first marriage was Alfred M. McGown, Stella's father. She was Dr. Prunty's third wife. Interestingly, his first, Mahalia, was the thirteenth child of Nathan Boone, and Mary's Aunt. Courtesy Ethelrose James.

Mary Boone Hosman.

father's mother. Grandmother was a country woman, very plain in her black dress with her hair combed back severely into a knot at the back of her neck. She was the picture of the pioneer woman she was.

Her first husband had been a doctor. He had died young, during my father's infancy. Dr. Robert T.C. Prunty, her second husband, had become an invalid. It was difficult for him to get around, even with crutches, as he was quite heavy. So grandmother would do all of the calling on the sick. She carried her medical book and delivered babies and served as both doctor and nurse.[21] It was never too late nor too cold and stormy for Grandmother to answer a call to visit the sick. I could remember when she brought a baby to her home that was seriously ill with pneumonia, and pulled it through. She also ran the farm and bought and sold stock. She was the first woman I had ever seen ride a horse man-fashion, in overalls. She would ride over the farm to mend fences. She would doctor a sick animal with the same patience she gave to the country folk.

Grandmother Prunty had often taken me, when I was a child, to visit her mother on the old Nathan Boone homestead in Missouri. My Great Grandmother Mary Hosman, who was the daughter of Nathan Boone and granddaughter of Daniel Boone, was the mother of thirteen children, and she was a good sturdy pioneer woman herself. Long after all her other children had grown and left home, she stayed on with her son, Robert, and managed the place with only his help.

I loved my Grandmother Prunty dearly, and I loved all my family, my parents, my brothers and sisters, my aunts and uncles and cousins. Mine had been a happy childhood, warm and secure in the comfortable cocoon of family affection.

Now, so suddenly, much sooner than I had intended, I had grown up and exchanged the old familiar ties for a new

Dr. Robert C. Prunty. Courtesy Ethelrose James.

family, a family I scarcely knew.

And I had become mistress of my own home. Jesse's mother had been moved to a centrally heated apartment[21] and I had the cottage to myself all the long day while Jesse was occupied with his business in town.

I was very, very happy as soon as Jesse came home each night. But something seemed to be missing from my life now. After a while, I realized what it was. I was not accustomed to being alone.

I didn't have to be alone long. When the warm weather returned, Zee James wanted to come home. Mary came to care for her. [22] I had grown quite fond of Zee James, and was grateful for her company. We spent hours together. She did not talk to me of her life with Jesse James when he was a hunted man. She did talk a great deal about her children, about her hopes for Jesse, Jr.

She told me of how Jesse was not allowed to play with other children until after his father was killed. She said little Jesse would stand in the window and watch other children at play. Or, at other times, she would sit with her children as they would run and play with other children, always with a fence between them.

"Little Tim," as Jesse was called by his family, wanted a dog. Zee told me how, on her husband's last trip to Kearney to see his mother, a few days before he was killed, he had spent the night at the home of his half sister, Sallie

---

[21] On June 4th or 5th, 1900, a census taker listed Zee James, Mary, and Zee's sister, Sallie Sullivan, as living at 410 Landis Court, across from Stella's parents.

[22] A reporter for the *New York Herald* visited the Jameses at this time. Please see appendix.

Nicholson, [23] and how he had carried a small dog in his lap as he made the trip from Kearney back to St. Joseph, Missouri, on horseback, a distance of thirty-five or forty miles. Jesse, Jr. was not to have his dog for long. He had to part with it after his father was killed. [24] Zee wanted me to understand her son. He was temperamental and had been pampered and spoiled by his mother and sister, because he was the breadwinner. This had already been made apparent to me, the first night we spent in the cottage with Jesse's mother and sister.

Jesse had mentioned several times that he thought he would take a bath. Finally his sister took me aside and told me it would be my duty to prepare the bath water, lay out his clothes, put the collar and cuff buttons in his shirt and brush his shoes. She said that it had been her job, and now it would be mine. This was not hard for me to do, as I had been next to eldest in a large family, and had been trained to do things for the other children.

And soon, I was looking forward to doing things for children of my own.

[23] Sarah Louisa Samuel Nicholson, the half-sister of Frank and Jesse James, was born at the James Farm on December 26th, 1858. She married William Nicholson and lived on the northern part of the original farm which had been given to her by her mother, Zerelda James Samuel. She died on September 15th, 1915.

[24] This little dog was sold at auction on April 10th, 1882, one week after the death of Jesse James in St. Joseph. Please see footnote No. 7.

CHAPTER 6

A NEW FAMILY

During the next six months that Mother Zee James spent with us, I was expecting our first baby. She hoped it would be a girl and we would name her Lucy for her favorite sister, Lucy Francis Browder.

It was at Lucy's small home in Kearney, Missouri that she and Jesse were married, she said. She had first met Jesse when he had been taken off the riverboat, mortally ill, during a voyage down the Missouri River: a dying man who had been hunted and hounded by the Federals since the day he had surrendered, honorably and in all sincerity, at the war's end, already badly wounded. He had never recovered from those battle wounds, and, tired of running and hiding, he was now going home to die. When his family took him off the boat at Harlem, they took him to the home of John Mimms, who kept a boarding house there. He was nursed by his mother and his sister Susie and by Zee Mimms, John's daughter. [25]

Zee's real name was Zerelda. She had the same name

---

[25] Jesse James said he was wounded on May 15th, 1865 and surrendered on May 21st. He claimed his wound was so bad his surrender was never processed. On June 13th, 1865 he was sent by steamboat, first to the boarding house of his uncle, John Mimms, in Harlem, a small town across the Missouri River from Kansas City, then, on July 15th to Rulo, Nebraska where his mother and family were staying. He returned to Harlem on August 26th and was taken to the James Farm later. John N. Edwards, *A Terrible Quintette*, St Louis *Dispatch*, Nov. 11th, 1873. Please see appendix.

Five generations of Stella's family, circa 1901. Left to right; Alfred M. McGown, father; Lucille James, daughter; Mary F. Prunty, grandmother; Stella Frances McGown; Mary Boone Hosman, great-grandmother. Courtesy Ethelrose James.

as Jesse's mother so Jesse called her Zee, for short, and Zee she had remained, ever since.

Zee had nursed the young man from August until late October when at last he was strong enough to be moved and he begged to be taken to his old home near Kearney. When he left, it was agreed between him and Miss Zerelda Mimms that if he ever recovered, they would be married.

Jesse had recovered his health, but he was still a hunted man the day he and Zee gathered with members of their families, in Kearney, at the home of Zee's sister Lucy on April 24th, 1874, to be married. There were no guests at the wedding and the service was performed by Jesse's uncle, Rev. William James.

Zee told me something that had happened that night.

It had always been a secret, she said, but I think she will forgive me if I tell it here.

The wedding ceremony was just about to begin when they received word that two detectives were riding toward Kearney from Liberty, Missouri, a few miles away.

Everybody looked for a place to hide Zee. There just did not seem to be a hiding place in the small three-room house, until Jesse thought of the big fat feather bed.

Zee was small, and she was placed between the feather bed and the mattress with just enough space at the top for air. The bed was then made smooth again.

Jesse left by the back door to go to the barn at the home of a friend, where two horses had been left saddled and ready. He watched until the detectives were inside Lucy's house, and then rode by, making all the noise that a fast travelling horse could make. Headed in the direction of Liberty, he quickly disappeared into the darkness.

As soon as the detectives set out in pursuit, as they supposed, Jesse returned for a quick wedding. Then he and Zee left immediately on a hunted honeymoon.[26] This was the most Zee James had ever told me about her experiences as the wife of a hunted man, and I found it difficult to picture what it must have been like to have one's domestic life turned into a series of hasty moves under cover of night, one narrow escape after another.

Actually, I still knew very little of the Jesse James story. It was during our courtship that I had heard more about the notorious James boys than I had ever heard before. Now that I was married, I found that I could not understand the astonishment of friends and relatives. Increasingly mystified, I decided to do some research of my own.

I bought a paperback, a sensational blood and thun-

---

[26] Please see appendix.

Jesse James, 16-year-old guerrilla warrior. This famous picture was taken from an ambrotype made in Platte City, Mo., on July 10, 1864 after the capture of the town. It was Jesse's first raid. He is wearing his "guerrilla shirt" and trying hard to appear fierce. He was not left-handed; ambrotypes—photos made on glass—like tintypes, produced a reversed image. Courtesy Ethelrose James.

der thing of the worst kind. It was not easy to do my reading in privacy in our little cottage. I managed to snatch a few lines at a time, getting part way through the book. There were pictures; flamboyant drawings of the James boys riding with bridle reins in their teeth, guns in each hand, shooting right and left. In some pictures they were shown in the company of gun-women.

I would sit and talk to Zee James. She was gentle and soft-spoken and the mother of the man I loved.

I was a very confused eighteen year old bride. I could not reconcile this gentle woman with Jesse James the bandit. To be perfectly truthful, I never have been able to do so.

THE JAMES FAMILY

W hat kind of people did Jesse James come from? As reported in a family tree, the family of Mary "Polly" Poor, grandmother of Frank and Jesse James, came from England, and settled in Virginia.

Old court records in England, as well as Virginia, testify as to the standing of the James and Poor families. John James married Mary "Polly" Poor in 1807, moved to Kentucky, and settled near Adairville, Logan County. Their fifth child was Robert Sallee James, the father of Frank and Jesse James.

Robert James was born on July 17th, 1818. He graduated from Georgetown College, Kentucky, in June 1843 and received a Master of Arts Degree in 1847. He had been ordained as a Baptist Minister in 1839.

Two years before graduation, Robert met and married Zerelda Cole, who was a student in a Catholic convent in Lexington. They were married on December 28th, 1841.

Zerelda's great grandfather was Richard Cole, Sr. He left Virginia after his marriage and settled in Woodford County, Kentucky, in the 1780's. Richard, Jr.'s son James, was the father of Zerelda.

Zerelda's mother was Sarah Lindsay, whose family traces its connections back to an old Scottish family. David Herndon Lindsay, a colonel in the Confederate Army during the Civil War, and later a Kentucky State Senator was a cousin of Zerelda Cole. Vachel Lindsay the American poet, was related to Sarah Lindsay. Sarah and Richard's eldest child was Zerelda E., born January 29th, 1825 in Woodford County, Kentucky. Zerelda Cole's brother was Richard Jesse Cole, born November 29th, 1826. The name "Jesse" appears several times in the Cole and Lindsay family trees. Zerelda's father was accidentally killed on February 27th, 1827, when she was very small. Her mother later married Robert Thomason and moved to Missouri. Zerelda stayed in Kentucky with her uncle, James M. Lindsay.

Robert and Zerelda James came to Missouri to visit Zerelda's mother, soon after they were married. They liked Missouri, and decided to make it their home.

Robert returned to Georgetown, Kentucky, to finish college, leaving Zerelda with her mother. He did not return to Missouri until after his graduation, in 1843.

Zerelda continued to live with her mother where their first son, Frank, was born on January 10th, 1843, while Robert was away at college.

In 1845, Robert & Zerelda bought a 275-acre farm nearby. This is where Jesse Woodson James was born on September 5th 1847, as well as Susan Lavinia James on November 25th, 1849.

Robert worked his farm during the week with the help of seven faithful negro servants. He was able to make a living for his family. He served God on Sunday as a preacher, but he was never paid for preaching.

Two of the churches he founded are still in existence today. They are the Providence Baptist Church in Clay County and the Pisgah Baptist Church near Excelsior Springs, Missouri.

He also re-organized the New Hope Baptist Church, not far from his farm.

"It has been said" wrote Robert Mimms and Lutie Mimms Gray, "that the old time preacher that served his congregation would surely have the most stars in his crown.

Such a preacher was Robert James, father of Frank and Jesse.

Membership in "New Hope" increased to 250. They came many miles from all directions. Many camped over the weekend once a month. It was the largest Baptist Church in Northwest Missouri".

Robert was also one of the founders of the William Jewell College in Liberty, Missouri where a painting of him hung in the halls until a few years ago.[27] Zerelda James Samuel told me she saw her husband Robert baptize as many as sixty-five people on one occasion, and of holding her young son, Jesse, up in her arms to view the baptisms.

Jesse was baptized near the same place years later, after he returned from the Civil War.

The violent history of Jesse and Frank James would never have been written had not their father the Reverend James, left his wife and three small children to join a wagon train, on a trip to the gold fields of California on April 12th, 1850 to preach to the miners for a year.

I have heard Zerelda James Samuel tell about how little Jesse clung to his father and pleaded with him not to go away. This affected the Rev. James very much. He told his wife that if he had not already spent so much money outfitting for the trip, and if he had not promised the men who were going with him, he would give up going.

This trip to California took four months. The men arrived there on August 1st, 1850. Rev. James died just three weeks later on August 18th 1850, in a small mining town

---

[27] It was later donated to the James Farm, by the college, and presently hangs there.

called Hangtown.[28] His widow, Zerelda Cole James, married Dr. Reuben Samuel on September 12th, 1855. They had four children: Sarah L. Samuel, Born December 26th, 1858 (married William Nicholson, November 28th, 1878); John T. Samuel, Born December 25th, 1861 (married Norma L. Maret, July 22nd, 1885); Fannie Quantrell Samuel, born October 18th, 1863 (married Joseph Hall, December 30th, 1880); and Archie Peyton Samuel, born July 26th, 1866 and murdered on January 26th, 1875 by detectives.

At the outbreak of the Civil War, there were a great many Southern families living in Clay County, Missouri, near the eastern border of Kansas, while Eastern Kansas was filled with Abolitionists who formed bands, called "Jayhawkers" by the Southern people.

Jayhawkers often invaded western Missouri before the Civil War. Feelings were very intense along the Missouri/Kansas border when the war began in 1861.

In the Spring of 1863, a band of Union militiamen came to the Samuel home looking for Frank James who had joined Quantrell's Confederate guerrilla organization. Zerelda Samuel, being a native of Kentucky, was naturally a Southern sympathizer, as was her husband, Dr. Reuben Samuel, and they had been visited before by northern soldiers and spies who asked many questions.

These militiamen, after questioning the women of the house, went out into the field where Jesse James and Dr. Samuel were plowing. Some of them took Dr. Samuel from the plow and drove him at the point of bayonets to a tree,

---

[28]Jesse James, Jr. made several unsuccessful trips to locate his grandfather's grave in this town, which was later called Placerville. His daughter, Josephine James Ross, also tried to locate the grave many years later, also in vain. (Author's Note). Frank and Jesse James had attempted to locate their father's grave in 1868 without success, and this editor tried as well in 1988. Homer Croy, *Jesse James Was My Neighbor.* (New York, 1949), 20.

where they put a rope around his neck and hanged him from a limb until he was nearly dead.

Then, lowering him they loosened the rope and demanded that he tell them where Frank James was. Three times they did this. Dr. Samuel could not tell them. He did not know.

Meanwhile, some of the other militiamen drove young Jesse, who was just fifteen years old, up and down the corn rows, lashing his back with a rope and threatening him with bayonets.

They forced him to watch the hanging of his step-father. They took the half-dead Dr. Samuel to the house and told Mrs. Samuel to bid her husband good-bye. He was found next day in the jail at Liberty, the county seat.

When the militiamen had gone, Jesse went to his mother, took his shirt off, and showing her the lacerations on his back, told her that this would never happen to him again.

Later he left home, a boy of fifteen, and joined the guerrillas.

Soon after this, Mrs. Samuel and her daughters were arrested, taken to St. Joe, Missouri, and placed in jail where they were kept for twenty-five days.

Jesse was badly wounded in the closing days of the war. In 1868 when he was able to travel, he went to California where he spent several months with his uncle Drury Woodson James. When his health improved he returned to his home, hoping to live the good life. He became converted, confessed his sins, and was baptized into the Baptist church.

In his book, *Noted Guerrillas or Warfare of the Border*, Major John N. Edwards observed:

"Jesse James had a face as smooth and as innocent as the face of a school girl. The blue eyes—very clear and penetrating—were never at rest. His form—tall and finely

molded—was capable of great endurance. On his lips there was always a smile, and for every comrade a pleasing word or compliment. Looking at his small white hands with their long tapering fingers, it was not then written or recorded that they were to become with a revolver among the quickest and deadliest in the West. [29]

This was the father of the man I married and these were the people who made up part of the family heritage of the next child who would be born to the James name:my child.

---

[29] John N. Edwards, *Noted Guerrillas or Warfare on the Border*, (St. Louis, 1877) 167-168.

CHAPTER 8

ZEE JAMES

Zee James, the widow of Jesse James, passed away on November 13th, 1900. Zerelda James was the daughter of John Mimms, a staunch Southerner from Scott County, Kentucky, who came from a highly respected family. She came to Missouri as a small girl. The family traveled down the Ohio and the Mississippi and Missouri rivers in a small boat. They landed on the north side of the Missouri River at a small place called Harlem. This was just across the river from Westport Landing, which is now Kansas City.

Her funeral eulogy was given by Rev. M.B. Chapman, of the Troost Avenue Methodist Episcopal Church, of which she was a member,

The pall bearers were men who had defended young Jesse at his trial. They were: R.L. Yeager, Frank P. Walsh, F.C. Farr, T.T. Crittenden Jr., E.P. Swinney and L.S. Banks.

The body was placed in a vault at Elmwood Cemetery to await removal to Kearney, where it was to be placed beside the grave of her husband, Jesse Woodson James.

Mary, Jesse and I had attended Mrs. James through her long illness, watching helplessly as she wasted away to a pathetic seventy pounds. The doctors had seemed unable to help her or even diagnose her illness.[30] Personally, I believed that Zee James had died of a broken heart. She had

---

[30]Please see appendix.

suffered a complete breakdown following the arrest and trial of her son, Jesse, Jr. She had been a devoted and courageous mother who had guided her children tenderly and watched over them prayerfully, determined that they should grow up respected citizens. Then, like a flash out of the past, there had come the bold headlines in the newspapers: **"JESSE JAMES, JR., ARRESTED FOR TRAIN ROBBERY!"** Zee James had not been able to recover from this shock. It had been her last heartbreak.[31] During the months that followed, my grief over the death of my husband's beloved Mother was mingled with my joy over the birth of our adorable baby daughter, Lucy, (Lucille Martha) who was born a month later, on December 21st 1900.

We gave Zee's first granddaughter the name she had requested: Lucille, after Zee's favorite sister, Lucy.

On June 29th, 1902, Mrs. James' body was removed to the Mt. Olivet Cemetery, in Kearney, and Jesse James' body was removed from the grave in his mother's yard where it had been buried at the time of his death in April of 1882. It was a private affair, with just a few of the friends and the immediate family.

Jesse, Jr. was in charge of the burial. It was a gloomy day, as somber as the occasion itself. It had started to rain early in the morning, and rained steadily during the opening of Jesse's grave by the undertaker and his helpers.

This took place in the forenoon. Jesse, Jr., was at the grave–side all during the opening. The body itself had completely disintegrated, as had the coffin. The skull and skeleton bones were all in place. The dark hair and beard

---

[31] "Just think", she told a reporter, "that by his arrest all my work for 22 years has been torn down and put to naught. How I guarded and watched that boy in order that no stigma could be discovered on his character. And how he obeyed me always…They arrest my boy because his names was *(sic)* Jesse James. That is what I have prayed against…for years." Kansas City *World*, October 12th, 1899.

Stella with Lucille, 1901. Courtesy Ethelrose James.

were perfect. The black suit was in splendid condition.

Jesse, Jr., picked up the skull of his father and examined it closely. He found the hole in the back of the head behind the right ear. I knew, when he told me about it later, that it had taken a great deal of strength to compel himself to give his father's remains this grim scrutiny; and I knew, too, that it was necessary:at the time of the murder, there had been rumors that Jesse had not really been killed but had only played a trick on the authorities.

Mrs. Samuel was not at the farm during this ordeal. She had gone to Kearney and was at the hotel with Frank James, who was ill with influenza. Frank had arrived several days before, but was unable to come out in the rain.

The skull and bones of Jesse James were placed in a black coffin with silver mounting and name plate. When this task was over, the casket was carried into the house to await the trip to Kearney in the afternoon.

The pall bearers were men who had served with Jesse under Quantrill. They were: Hi George, W.A. Gregg, J. Frank Gregg, Warren Welch, Sam Whitsett, and Hicks George.[32] Two photographers had been optimistic enough to wade through the rain and deep mud to come to the farm, but with the steady downpour of rain, I doubt that they got a picture before late afternoon when the sun came out for a moment. I later saw in the newspapers a picture that had been taken at the cemetery.

Jesse, Jr., returned to Kearney to join his Uncle Frank and his grandmother at the hotel. Frank was host to the pall bearers, his mother and Jesse, Jr., at a country dinner at the small hotel. I did not go into Kearney but remained at the farm with our six month old baby.

After dinner, there were several buggies, one carriage, and all the horses that were available from the livery stable,

---

[32] Please see appendix.

Original marker on Jesse James' grave, Mt. Olivet Cemetery, Kearney, Missouri. Damage seen here caused by souvenir hunters eventually disfigured the monument so badly that Jesse's daughter had it removed and supposedly destroyed. However, the carved obelisk base was discovered in 1988 and is now in the Museum at the James Farm.

to make the trip out to the farm. The hearse arrived just ahead of them and was waiting at the farm to take Jesse James to his last burial place beside his faithful wife.

The large white stone monument that had been placed at the grave in the yard of Mrs. Samuel was now taken to Kearney Cemetery. But here, in a location that was accessible to the general public, this solemn monument was subjected to unscrupulous desecration by souvenir hunters and was gradually chipped away.[33]

[33] Jesse's daughter Mary purchased a house adjoining the cemetery, in an effort to protect her father's monument from further destruction. After Mary's death, the monument was destroyed. It was replaced in June, 1960. (Author's note) In 1988 the base of the original monument bearing the inscription was discovered by the editor. It is now on exhibition at the James Farm Museum. The grave was marked with a Confederate veteran's headstone on August 5th, 1989.

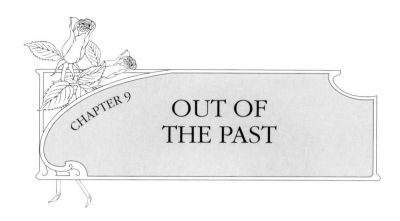

CHAPTER 9

OUT OF THE PAST

For awhile, Mary James seemed at a loss, now that she no longer had her mother to nurse and care for. Though she seemed to enjoy playing with her new niece, little Lucille, she was obviously not at peace. It was as if she no longer felt needed, and could not make up her mind what to do with her life.

By the following spring, a young farmer from around Kearney, Henry Barr, made up her mind for her by making her his wife.

The wedding was held on March 6th, 1901 at the home of Jesse's Aunt, Sallie Nicholson, who was the half-sister of Jesse James. Though it was still too soon after the death of Zee for the wedding to be an altogether festive occasion, we were all happy for Mary, especially Jesse and I. We knew, better than anyone else except Zee herself, what a devoted daughter Mary had been, and we wanted to see her find contentment now in a home and family of her own.

Aunt Sallie's farm was near the old James home. Jesse and I were to spend the night with her before returning to our own home in Kansas City. The day's excitement had tired me a bit, and I knew it would not take me long to fall asleep that night. But after the wedding guests departed, Aunt Sallie, an energetic, intelligent woman much like her mother, Zerelda Samuel, wanted to sit and talk with Jesse, Jr., whom she did not get to see very often.

When the three of us were alone, Aunt Sallie had her young son go out to the barn and fetch a little dog that had

Sallie Samuel Nicholson—the "Aunt Sallie" Stella and Jesse, visited. She was Jesse James' half-sister and her husband was one of Jesse's closest friends.

been kept out there during the wedding.

The dog, a cute little brown and white spotted fellow, seemed very glad to be back in the house among friends. He chased around, wagging his tail, coming to Jesse and me to be petted before jumping on Aunt Sallie's lap.

Scratching the little dog's ears, Aunt Sallie said to Jesse,

"Did you know that Spot, here, is the son of the great grand-daughter of the mother of the little dog I gave you twenty years ago?"

Jesse grinned. "The dog you gave me?" he repeated. "Do you mean the dog my father brought to me on horseback all the way from your house that night, the night of his last visit home?"

Aunt Sallie nodded. "That's right. He carried the pup under his coat to protect him from the snow. He'd been telling me how much you wanted a dog, and I said, well, why shouldn't he have one? Every little boy should have a dog! And we picked out that pup for you. Of course, I knew your life wasn't like other little boy's, having to move all the time, not allowed to play with other children. But your Daddy was just sure things were going to be different from then on. He'd just brought you and your mother and sister to St. Joe, and he had big plans for you. Real nice plans."

As she said this, Aunt Sallie's eyes misted a little. She dug down in her pocket for a handkerchief, blew her nose vigorously, and then went on patting the dog in her lap.

"Tell me about his plans, Aunt Sallie," Jesse urged. "Tell me everything you can remember about that visit and the things you and father talked about."

I was sitting beside Jesse on Aunt Sallie's old horsehair sofa. It was all I could do to keep my tired head from dropping down on the comfortable pillow of my husband's broad shoulder. But Jesse was wide awake now, and I could sense his eager alertness as he questioned Aunt Sallie.

"Oh, I warned your Daddy that night," Aunt Sallie was saying. "I told him about the danger to him and Zee and you children in his coming back to Missouri. Why, some of the men who had been good friends and neighbors, themselves good Southern people and in sympathy with the cause Jesse and Frank had left home to fight for, those same men were spies now, working with the sheriffs and detectives to try

and capture him. I warned him!...you know what he said?"
Jesse was listening intently.

Aunt Sally went on:"He just laughed and said he reckoned he'd have to win the friendship of those people all over again when he came home to stay!" She shook her head and sighed. "He said he was sure our Mother and our friends would win their plea to the Governor to have him surrender and stand trial. He said that if he was convicted he would go ahead and serve his time. At least then his family would be free to live at home in Missouri. And if he were acquitted, he'd build a home on his land and live as a human being should. That's all he'd ever really wanted, Jesse, and he wanted it more than ever for you and Mary and your mother...."

Jesse said quietly, as if to himself, "It was not to be...."

Aunt Sallie burst out, "Those Ford boys! How could any of us have known what they were plotting in their sneaky cowardly minds?"

"Did you talk to them that night?" Jesse asked quickly.

Aunt Sallie shook her head.

"They didn't spend the night here?" Jesse prompted.

"Not in this house they didn't. Of course, I knew there was someone with Jesse, all right, but he didn't bring them in, and I never learned until later that it was the Ford brothers. Figured then that they must have slept in the schoolhouse. They could have built a fire out there and kept warm...." [34] The talk between Jesse, Jr., and his aunt went on through the night. Presently I dozed, but still caught snatches of the conversation from time to time.

Aunt Sallie had given Jesse, Jr., letters to read with clippings from newspapers charging his father with crimes committed hundreds of miles away from where he'd actually been at the time.

---

[34] See Appendix.

After a while, I heard the roosters crow to announce the breaking of day. With my head cradled on Jesse, Jr.'s shoulder, I opened one eye to see that the little dog in Aunt Sallie's lap was contentedly snoozing, too, unmindful of the earnest conversation between his mistress and her nephew.

Aunt Sallie was saying that there were great differences in disposition between Jesse and Frank James, that Jesse was of a happy and generous nature while Frank was more serious and inclined to be selfish at times.

"One time," she said, "when Jesse and Frank returned home, Jesse brought us some beautiful silk he'd bought in New York. He said it was for dresses for Sister Fannie and me. Of course, it was far too expensive for dresses to be worn in the country. But we loved him for it, he was always doing things like that for us. Another time he went to Kansas and bought me a real nice saddle, finest leather, hand tooled. I've still got it. I don't recall that Frank ever gave any of us a gift…." [35] I was drifting off to sleep again when Jesse suddenly exclaimed, "What time is it getting to be? Why, it's daybreak! This poor girl of mine must get some rest!"

"Why, the poor child!" Aunt Sallie cried. "We've kept her up the whole night long. What a pair of talking fools we are! We'd best get Stella to bed if she's ever going to be fit to make the trip home today."

After a few hours' peaceful slumber in the big four-poster bed in Aunt Sallie's spare bedroom, I was refreshed and ready for the journey back to Kansas City. Jesse, Jr., had rested for a while, too, but his mind was still on the long talk of the night before, and during the trip he explained some of it to me.

[35] Jesse also gave his little half-brother Archie Peyton Samuel a wood recorder. Archie was killed by the explosion on January 26th, 1875. Zerelda gave it to Sally's son, Arch Nicholson who was named for her brother. His son, John, presented it to the James Farm Museum on August 5th, 1989.

"You heard Aunt Sally mention my father's belief that he was going to be allowed to surrender so that his family could finally settle down and live in peace and freedom. My grandmother and friends of the family went to three different governors of Missouri and begged and pleaded for terms on which my father could surrender. These overtures were spurned.

"My father was anxious to surrender at all times. He told his mother a short time before he died that he would be willing to wear duck clothing [36] for the rest of his life if only he could be a free man. All of this pleading for a chance to surrender were in vain. His old enemies were working constantly to prejudice the public against him.

"I have looked through the old files of the Kansas City daily papers and other papers published during those years, and it is ridiculous to see what crimes were charged up to the account of my hunted and outlawed father. This week there would be a bold robbery somewhere in Missouri and the newspapers would print in big headlines that it had been the James gang. The next week there would be a robbery in Texas, and again it would be the James gang. To have committed one-fourth of these crimes that were charged against him, my father would have to have been equipped with an airship or some means of extra-terrestrial transportation to have made it possible for him to rob a bank in West Virginia Monday night, and hold up a train in Texas three nights later.

"The very day on which my father was killed, there was a particularly bold and successful hold-up and robbery of a train in Texas, and the newspapers all over the country attributed it to Jesse James!.

"Anyone who doubts this is true can turn to the files of

---

[36] Rough apparel made from canvas and usually worn only by laborers.

the daily newspapers of that date and prove it for himself as it appears right in the first page of most of the papers." [37] As further evidence of his father's sincere desire to provide his family with a decent, normal life, Jesse, Jr., told me about a letter his father had written in answer to an ad offering a farm for sale.

Jesse James had truly yearned to buy that farm for his wife Zee and his two small children. Of his sincerity there can be no doubt, as I later saw for myself when I had an opportunity to examine copies of both the ad[38] and the letter, which read as follows:

The advertisement:

FOR SALE—a very fine 160 acres, adjoining the town of Franklin, Franklin Co. Corners with depot ground. Living springs; beautiful creek runs through it. 90 acres in body of finest bottom land: balance natural young timber. Mill within a mile. As good educational, religious, railroad and other facilities as any point in western Nebraska. $10 per acre. Address or call on J.P. Calhoun, Lincoln Neb. Feb15 d6&wlt.

[37] An examination of a number of newspapers for April 3-4th, 1882 has failed to substantiate this claim.

[38] *Lincoln (Nebraska) Journal,* Feb. 15th, 1882. The letter was reproduced in J.A. Dacus, *Illustrated Lives and Adventures of Frank and Jesse James and the Younger Brothers, the Noted Western Outlaws.* (St. Louis, 1882).

Jesse's letter:

Mr. J.D. Calhoun
Lincoln Neb
Dear Sir,
    I have noticed that you have 160 acres of land adver-tised for sale in Franklin Co. Neb. Please write at once and let me know the lowest cash price that will buy your land. Give me a full description of the land etc.
    I want to purchase a farm of that size provided I can find one to suit. I will not buy a farm unless the land is No.1.
    I will start on a trip in about 8 days to Northern Kansas and South Nebraska and if the description of the land suits me I will look at it & if it suits me I will buy it from the advertisement in the Lincoln Journal. I suppose your land can be made a good farm for stock and grain—Please answer at once.
Respectfully
Tho. Howard
No.1318 Lafayette St.
St. Joseph Mo
March 2nd '82'

    Jesse James had been making, as Aunt Sallie said, "real nice plans" for his little family.
    But before he could buy the farm, Jesse James was dead.

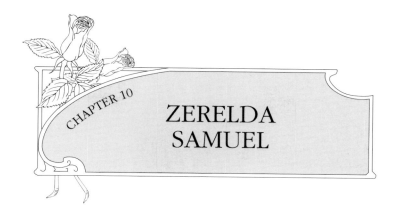

CHAPTER 10

ZERELDA SAMUEL

I had met Jesse, Jr.'s grandmother, Mrs. Zerelda Samuel, briefly, during the summer before our marriage, when she was visiting in the home of Jesse, Zee and Mary. Large of stature, robust, dignified, she was about 75 years of age at the time, but not an old woman by any means.

Now, during the next few years, through frequent visits, I became better acquainted with Zerelda Samuel, mother of Frank and Jesse James.

She had seen trouble and tragedy enough to have broken any woman of lesser spirit. She had been left a widow with three small children by the Rev. Robert James when he died in California in 1850.[39] On September 12th, 1855, Zerelda married Dr. Reuben Samuel and mothered a second family of four children.[40] She had lived through a cruel and bloody War Between the States that resulted in two of her sons becoming hunted men, branded as outlaws; a war that also resulted in her hand being blown off and her youngest child being killed by a bomb that was thrown into her home at night by Pinkerton detectives who were seeking to kill or capture her "outlaw" sons.

What the good Lord had denied this woman in happiness and a peaceful life, He seemed to have made up for by providing her with a remarkable sense of humor, in dark

---

[39] Please see appendix.

[40] Please see appendix.

Zerelda Cole James Simms Samuel, mother of Frank and Jesse James. Fiercely loyal to her sons, she defended them until her death in 1911. Her life was filled with tragedy: her first husband died when she was the young mother of three little children; her second marriage failed quickly; her last husband was tortured during the Civil War and died in an asylum; her second child died an infant; another, Archie, was killed in an explosion during a raid by detectives on her house; her oldest were the most wanted outlaws of all and Jesse was murdered in his own home. James Farm Collection.

Mrs. Zerelda Samuel, mother of Frank and Jesse James, with a group of tourists at her home, the James Farm. Tourists started visiting the Farm after Jesse's death in 1882, making it one of the oldest continually operated historic sites in Missouri. Built in 1822, the house is one of the oldest inhabited structures between western Missouri and California. James Farm Collection.

times as well as in good times.

Her abundant comic spirit was ever at hand. Mrs. Samuel was intelligent, and she had the bearing of an educated woman.[41] After Jesse was killed, people came by the hundreds to visit the home of the James boys and to meet their mother. People from all walks of life came. There were governors, statesmen, writers and just plain people.

The James Farm is near Excelsior Springs, Missouri,

---

[41] She had attended St. Catherine's Academy, Lexington, Kentucky and was a student there when she met Robert James.

Members of the Samuel family in the yard of the home, circa 1886. Left to right: Dr. Reuben Samuel; Perry Samuel, a former slave; Mrs. Zerelda Samuel and Norma Maret Samuel, wife of John Samuel, son of Reuben and Zerelda. James Farm Collection.

then a famous health resort, with several large hotels. The livery stable had regular scheduled trips to the farm each day. Others came in private rigs.[42] Mrs. Samuel liked to meet people and tell her story. She had what she called a "memory cane." Visitors would send her a ribbon to tie on the cane, with their names, addresses, and dates of their visits on them. Many ribbons were fancy, expensive ribbons with names embossed in gold; others were hand embroidered. There were hundreds of these ribbons.[43] The mother of

[42] Over 3,500 people visited the James Farm between 1895 and 1898. *Kansas City Star,* October 12th, 1898. Please see appendix.

[43] They have since been donated to the James Farm Museum by the family of Jesse James, Jr.

Frank and Jesse James was strong-willed and had plenty of determination. From the very beginning of her marriage to Rev. Robert James in Kentucky, she had servants. Aunt Charlotte, who had been a slave in Zerelda's family, came to Missouri with Robert and Zerelda and had remained with them after the war. After I became a member of the family, I heard a great deal about Aunt Charlotte, and about another of the James' colored servants, Ambrose.

When I came into the family, however, there was just one servant left; Perry. I never knew just when or how he had become part of the family, but he seemed to have always "belonged," and was called Perry Samuel. He was about thirty-four or thirty-five when I met him in 1900.

Zerelda Samuel had always given orders, but she had never taken any. Dr. Samuel was a small, meek and quiet man, and I suspected that Zerelda had always "worn the pants."

I also suspected that Mrs. Samuel had never missed a chance to play a joke on someone-and indeed, I was to become a victim of some of her pranks, as time went on.

In any case, Perry was apparently accustomed to her ways, and he managed her home very smoothly for her. He was farm-hand, cook, houseboy and maid for her, and drove for her whenever she needed to leave the farm.

Then the day came when Perry took himself a wife and left the James Farm to establish a home of his own. Zerelda was like a "ship without a rudder" after Perry married. She could not seem to keep help on the farm during the winter. Jesse, Jr., sent several couples over from the city, but the longest any of them stayed was three weeks. Mrs. Samuel could not understand why she should have to pay and feed two people to do the work one had done all these many years.

She decided she would close her home for the winter and go and live in Kearney. There were two hotels in

Kearney, and she tried both; then a private home. Then a call was made for Jesse, Jr., to send another couple to the farm- only to repeat the whole cycle a few weeks later. [44] "Why don't we have her come here?" I asked Jesse finally. "Our home is certainly big enough. I can get a cook and house- keeper. And I know Aunt Sallie would be glad to come and stay with us for a while. She's always been such a wonderful help with the children."

I meant our other Aunt Sally, (Sarah Ann Sullivan) sister of Jesse, Jr.'s mother, Zee James. A widow, she often came to spend some time with us. Our daughters adored her.

Jesse, Jr., agreed that with Aunt Sally to help with the children, I would be free to give Zerelda the care she needed. So it was decided. And Zerelda arrived, bag and baggage, in the middle of December.

Things went along nicely, for a while. Then the cook left. I couldn't blame her. Grandma would order a meal, then suddenly sometimes change the order just before mealtime. Moreover, since she had always been ready for company at all times in her own home, she would be here. She would change into her black alpaca dress and large white bow tie, every afternoon. This tie was always either too stiff, or not stiff enough. She had lost one hand, and never had to learn to use the one she had, to do things for herself. Aunt Sally and I were kept busy!

It was during this time that I became the victim of one of Zerelda's famous jokes. Frank Nicholson and his wife, Effie, came over from Kearney for a visit. Frank's mother was Sallie Nicholson, Mrs. Samuel's daughter. One evening, Jesse, Frank, Effie and I went to the theatre. Grandma was not entirely happy that we should go out, instead of staying

[44] Please see appendix.

Stella James poses on the porch of her home at 809 Elmwood, Kansas City. Her daughters and other children are on the grass. Courtesy Ethelrose James.

and visiting with her. I suspect she lay awake thinking of a way to get even, for she did just that, before we went to bed that night.

In the after-theatre rush to board a streetcar, Effie and I got on the car just as the door was closed, leaving our husbands to take another car. This was not bad until I learned that we had taken the Independence, Missouri car, when we should have taken the Independence Avenue car.

This meant a long ride back, and a cross-town transfer. [45]

Effie, being a country girl and unaccustomed to being on the streets at night, was sure we would be killed by thugs before we could reach home.

We had expected to find our husbands at home, worried about us. We found instead a dark house and no husbands.

Grandma and Aunt Sally were sharing a downstairs room, and I went to inquire if there had been a telephone call. There had not been but Grandma had a suggestion. It was that we turn off the lights, sit in the dark, and wait for them. They would believe that we were not at home.

Effie was too upset to go to bed anyway, and we went along with Grandma's joke. By two o'clock in the morning, Effie was on the verge of a collapse. She was sure that Frank and Jesse had met with foul play, or else that they were stepping out to see some night life, a thought that seemed equally distressing to her.

As for me, I was getting madder by the minute. And then Aunt Sallie could stand the strain no longer. She came to tell us that our husbands had come home two hours earlier, and, at Grandma's suggestion, had gone upstairs to bed, to let us worry about them!

I marched into Grandma's room with the intention of letting off a little steam. I found her laughing heartily, thoroughly enjoying her little joke.

I said good night, and went up to bed.

Poor Dr. Samuel had often been the victim of his wife's jokes. I was told of one that almost proved fatal to him. This was during the visit of a relative by the name of George

---

[45] The Jameses lived at 809 Elmwood at that time, a house that has been restored.

Dr. Reuben Samuel, beloved step-father of Frank and Jesse James. James Farm Collection.

James, who was spending a few days at the farm. [46] George reported to Zerelda that he had seen something moving in the bushes near the grave when he went up to the little "Chick Sale" (outhouse) in the garden. The grave referred to was that of Jesse James.

Mrs. Samuel told her husband of George's report and suggested that the doctor hide in the bushes the next night to scare George and find out how he would react to such a fright.

The following night, Dr. Samuel was sent out to hide in

[46] George James, the son of Rev. William. In 1875 he was apprehended at the farm with Ed Miller and Ed Samuel, half brother of Reuben, and accused of "being pickets" for the James brothers. *Kansas City Times,* January 28th, 1875.

Zerelda Samuel standing at Jesse James' grave in the yard of her home at the old family farm. The body and monument were moved to the family plot in Mr. Olivet Cemetery in nearby Kearney, Mo. in 1902. James Farm Collection.

the bushes, with a sheet over him. When he had been out in the cold night for a long time, Zerelda asked George to go out in the garden to see if the doctor was all right. She said she feared he might have taken sick out there.

What she did not know was that George was a firm believer in self-protection: on his way out, George picked up a large stick of stove wood from the back porch, and he was about to give the doctor a sound beating that night before he could get himself untangled from the sheet and the bushes and explain that it was all just one of Zerelda's jokes.

One very hot night while we were visiting Grandma

Samuel, the children were unable to sleep inside. We made a bed for them out under the big tree in the yard, very near the grave of Jesse James. The children did not want to be left alone so I lay down by the side of their bed and fell asleep. I awoke to find I had rolled down a slight slant and was sleeping on top of the grave of Jesse James. This may not be a distinction, but I doubt that there is another person who can say they slept on the grave of Jesse James!

The last time I saw Dr. Samuel was when Jesse and I went over to the farm at the request of John Samuel [47] who wanted to talk to Jesse about his father. John said Zerelda thought the doctor might be losing his mind: he had struck her!

While Perry was preparing dinner, I went to see if I could help. Perry asked me if I would make the biscuits. He said that Dr. Samuel had always made them, but the doctor had "gone on strike." [48] I asked Perry if the doctor was sick. Perry replied, "Does he look sick, just sitting there on the porch, rocking himself?"

I then asked him if he thought the doctor was losing his mind. Perry said, "No, I think he just found it!" [49]

After the Pinkerton detectives threw the bomb into the Samuel home on January 26th, 1875, that killed her eight-year-old son Archie, and tore Mrs. Samuel's hand off, they were tracked in the snow through the fields to a spur of the railroad at Kearney, where a one car special had been left

[47] John T. Samuel, half brother of Frank and Jesse James.

[48] "Dr. Samuels *(sic)* ... is one of the best house keepers *(sic)* in Missouri. He can cook, bake, wash and iron...he always gets the breakfast and supper ... There is not a cleaner house in Missouri .... *Bowling Green* (Missouri) *Times.* (August 21st, 1890).

[49] Dr. Samuel died in the State Insane Asylum, St. Joseph, Missouri on March 1st, 1908.

waiting to take them away. They had lost a gun in the Samuel's yard, with the initials "PGG" for Pinkerton Government Guard stamped on it.

The press made much of the cowardly deed, and a great deal of criticism was expressed of the Pinkerton Agency and of the railroad that took the detectives out to the farm and brought them back.

It seemed that, as a result, Mrs. Samuel was given a lifetime pass on that railroad for herself and her entire family.

Mrs. Samuel made good use of that pass. When she expected to make a trip to Kansas City, she would let it be known to all of the relatives who might like to go to the city. She would take any and all who wanted to go. If only a few showed up at the station, she would find neighbors and friends to take along on her pass.

We had come to know the conductor on the train, as we made frequent trips to Kearney. He told us that whenever he saw a large crowd at the station, he would expect to find Mrs. Samuel in the midst of it. He said the officials of the railroad knew of Mrs. Samuel's "adopted family" on these trips, but they made no objection.

Grandma Samuel spent a part of her last winter in our home, before she went to Fletcher, Oklahoma to visit her son Frank. She died on her way back to Kearney.

Frank's wife, Anna, was with her at the time. After suffering from a heart-stroke, Zerelda had been taken off the train at Oklahoma City. There she died on February 10th, 1911.

Mrs. Samuel was buried at Mt. Olivet Cemetery near the graves of Dr. Samuel, Archie, Zee and Jesse.[50] In all the stories I have read and the movies I have seen about the James family, Mrs. Samuel has been portrayed as an unedu-

---

[50] Please see appendix

cated, uncouth, mean person. Such a picture is completely false.

Had Zerelda Samuel lived in our day, she could well have been a leader among women. She fought for what she believed in, and, like a general, once she was in the fight, she gave her all.

This seems to be a good place to include the official report of Adjutant General George C. Bingham to the Senate and Governor Charles H. Hardin, of Missouri.

"Dear Sir: In pursuance of instructions received from you on Friday last, I proceeded without delay to Clay County to ascertain, as far as possible, the facts relating to the recent outrages perpetrated in said county upon said family of, *(sic)* the step-father of the notorious James brothers, and to cooperate with the authorities there in any proper effort to bring the perpetrators to justice.

"Having no power to compel witnesses to testify under oath, I have been able to obtain little information beyond that which has already been given to the public by the press.

"Mr. Samuels *(sic)* resides about 2½ miles east of Kearney, a small town 9 miles north of Liberty, and located on a branch of the H.& St. Jo R.R. (Hannibal and St. Joseph Railroad) running from Kansas City to Cameron. On the night of January 26th (1875) between 12:00 and 2:00 o'clock, the residence of Mrs. Samuels *(sic)* was approached by a party of men, the precise number of them is not known. A portion of the men stationed themselves behind an ice house on the east side of the house and in front of the dwelling, about fifty or sixty yards therefrom. Another portion went in the rear of the building, the same being in the form of the letter "L" containing two rooms; the one farthest from the main building serving as a kitchen and sleeping room for negro servants. The entire building is a weather boarded log structure, somewhat dilapidated by time. The party which approached the rear and west por-

The James Farm, Kearney, Missouri.

tion of the building set fire to the weather boarding of the kitchen in three of four places, and threw into the window a hand grenade.

"This instrument was composed of cast and wrought or malleable iron, strongly secured together and covered with a wrapping saturated with turpentine or oil. As it passed through the window and as it lay upon the floor, it made a very brilliant light, alarming the family who supposed the kitchen to be on fire and rushed in to extinguish the flames. Mr. Samuels, *(sic)* seeing the burning instrument upon the floor, mistook it for a turpentine ball and attempted to kick it into the fireplace. Failing in this on account of its weight, he seized a poker and a pair of iron tongs, by means of which, he succeeded in getting it into the fireplace. It then immediately exploded with a report that was heard a distance of two or three miles. The part composed of cast iron broke into fragments and flew out with great force. One of the fragments shattered the right arm below the elbow of Mrs. Samuels *(sic)* the mother of the James brothers, to an extent which made amputation necessary. Another entered the body of her little son, Archie, wounding him mortally and causing his death in a few hours.

"Mr. Samuels *(sic)* succeeded in putting out the fire in the weather–boarding, *(sic)* and arousing the surrounding neighbors with a cry of 'Murder' which he continued to repeat until he was exhausted. Four pistol reports were heard by the neighbors as they came toward the dwelling, but when they reached it, the parties perpetrating the outrage had disappeared.

WHO WERE THESE PARTIES?

"This is a question which yet finds no answer, except in circumstances which do not seem sufficient for a complete solution of the mystery. On Monday, January 26th, about half past seven o'clock in the evening, an engine with only a caboose attached came down the (rail)road from the north and stopped in the woods about two miles north of Kearney. Several unknown men got out of the caboose, which then continued south in the direction of Kansas City. About two or three o'clock in the morning, Tuesday, the same or a similar engine and caboose came from the direction of Kansas City and stopped for a considerable time at the place where the unknown men had been left after dark on the previous evening. The tracks of persons who were stationed behind the house and of those who set fire to and threw the grenade into the kitchen, and which were found on the path of their retreat, are made by boots of superior quality, quite different from those usually worn by farmers and farm hands in the surrounding country. In following the trail of the party on their retreat, a pistol was found which is now in my possession. The pistol has marks upon it which would scarcely be seen unless sought for, and which, I have been credibly informed, are identically such as are known to be on the pistols of a well known band of detectives.

THE BULLET HOLES

"The bullet holes found on the fence on the east side of the dwelling, of which frequent mention had been made, do not indicate a conflict. If discharged from the direction of the ice house the Samuel dwelling would have been out of their range, and it cannot be supposed that the James brothers, had they really been home, would have left the dwelling to expose themselves openly to a superior force under cover. There are seven of these holes, and all within a space of 18 inches or two feet. The neighbors who came to the house immediately after the alarm was given all concur in the statement that but five reports were heard, one very loud and the other four subsequent thereto and such as might be caused by discharges from pistols. Their impression is that this firing was for the purpose of keeping them at a distance until the assailants could make good their retreat. These bullet holes may be the result of some previous target shooting with pistols.

THE BLOOD

"A little blood was found in several places on the snow in the path of the assailants as they retreated from the dwelling, but not more than might be caused by an accidental scratch on the hand or by bleeding at the nose. The parties who perpetrated the outrage doubtless approached the house under the belief that the James brothers were there, and set fire to it and threw in the grenade for the purpose of forcing them out and then shooting or capturing them; and on discovering that they had murdered an innocent lad and mutilated his mother, they deemed it prudent to retire and leave as little evidence by which they could be traced and identified.

THE JAMES BOYS

"I could not learn from any reliable source that either

of the James boys had been in the area since last April. If they were in the house at the time they could have escaped through the cowardice of those attempting their capture. I had a correspondence of some length with Mrs. Samuels *(sic)* their mother. She has had the advantage of an early education, and seems to be endowed with a vigorous intellect and masculine will; but she could give no information bearing upon the object of my visit.

"I am satisfied that nothing short of the inquisitorial power of a Grand Jury is likely to elicit such evidence as will lead to the identification of the parties engaged in a transaction the nature of which naturally permits them to resort to every possible method of concealment.

"In the foregoing statement I have omitted the names of the citizens from whom I obtained such information as it contains, believing it best for the ends of justice that they should not be given to the public. I am convinced that the people of Clay County would feel greatly relieved if the James brothers could be captured and brought to justice. Their notoriety as desperados and the impunity which has accompanied their reckless doings are regarded as a most serious injury both to the character and material interests of their County, charged as it has been with affording them cover and protection.

Respectfully,
G.C. Bingham
Adjutant-General"

SPECIAL MESSAGE OF THE GOVERNOR
"The Governor transmitted to the Senate a special message, endorsing the report of the Adjutant-General, and says that in response to the resolutions adopted by the General Assembly he presents so much of General Bingham's report as may be made public, and he adds:
"Condemning as I do most severely such outrage upon

the peace and quiet of society it is my purpose to use all the power I possess to bring the offenders to trial. Some facts create a belief that persons, nonresidents of this State, have, without the requisite authority, raided into the State and undertaken in a wanton brutal and wicked way to accomplish some ulterior design they had in view on crossing into the State. Of course, requisitions for the return of such parties to the State will be made as soon as developments shall establish this fact, as well as the names of the parties. C.H. Hardin."[51]

---

[51] *Liberty Advance*, February 12th, 1875; *Jefferson City Peoples Tribune*, February 10th, 1875.

CHAPTER 11

FRANK JAMES

I met Frank James, for the first time, when he and his son Robert came to Kansas City to attend our wedding in January, 1900. He was living in St. Louis at the time.

Later, he bought a small farm in Fletcher, Oklahoma, where he lived with his faithful wife, Anna, until the time of his mother's death on February 10th, 1911.

He then returned to Kearney, to take over the family farm which Zerelda had maintained all these years.

Now that they were living in Kearney, Frank and Anna came to visit our family often. Jesse, Jr. and I now had four little daughters[52] and we all looked forward to Uncle Frank's visits.

Always, when he and Aunt Anna were traveling and needed to take a morning train out of Kansas City, they would come over on the afternoon train and spend the night in our home.

On one of Frank's visits with us, one of our daughters told him of seeing a cave in the Ozark Mountains of Missouri where Jesse and Frank were supposed to have hidden when they were being hunted.

Frank's typical reply was, "The Frank and Jesse James I knew never went into a place that they couldn't get out of by a back door."

---

[52] Lucille Martha (Dec. 21st, 1900-June 11th, 1988) Josephine Frances (April 20th, 1902-March 31st, 1964) Jessie Estelle (August 27th, 1906-February 2nd, 1987) Ethelrose (July 10th, 1908).

Alexander Franklin James in 1898. He surrendered to the Governor of Missouri in 1882 and was tried twice for various crimes and acquitted both times. He spent his last years on the old family farm and often visited Stella and Jesse, Jr. Courtesy Ethelrose James.

When talking to our daughters, Uncle Frank never referred to himself as Frank James, but always spoke of "The Frank James I knew." Jesse, Jr. called his Uncle Frank, "Uncle Ben;" that is the name he knew him by as a child.[53] Frank died on February 18th, 1915, and his funeral was held in his home at Kearney.

Anna James had always been retiring, and she became even more so after Frank's death.[54] People came from far and near to attend Frank's funeral. They came by special train from Kansas City; by automobile, and by farm rigs. But the funeral was private. No reporters were allowed.

The funeral oration was given by Judge John Phillips. Judge Phillips had been leading defense attorney for the trial of Frank James at Gallatin, Missouri, in 1883, after Frank had surrendered to Governor Crittenden on October 5th, 1882. As a result of this trial, Frank had been acquitted and was henceforth able to enjoy the rest of his life as a free man.[55]

[53] As a child, Jesse, Jr. knew his uncle by his alias "Ben Woodson" and retained the habit of calling him by that name, just as he was often called "Tim."

[54] Anna James never talked of her life with Frank James during his outlaw days, not even to the family. She had a standing offer for an attractive sum of money, from a leading magazine if she would tell her story. She was never interviewed, nor did she allow herself to be photographed. I remember well that after being invited to attend the wedding of our daughter, Jo Francis, on September 2nd, 1925, Anna failed to appear. Then I heard that she had been driven to our home by a relative, but when she saw a photographer carrying his camera into the house, she left without entering. (Author's footnote) Please see Appendix

[55] Frank James was tried in Gallatin, Missouri, August 21st- September 6th, 1883, for the Winston train robbery and the murder of a passenger. He was acquitted and then tried at Huntsville, Alabama, April 17-25th, 1884, for the robbery of the government paymaster at Muscle Shoals, Alabama, on March 11th, 1881. He was again acquitted. *Settle*, 152-153.

Annie Ralston James. College educated schoolteacher daughter of a well-to-do Independence, Missouri family, she eloped with Frank James in 1874 and shared his life as a wanted outlaw. James Farm Collection.

I was deeply moved, and I know Jesse, Jr. was, too, by the oration given by Judge Phillips at Frank James's funeral:

"Friends:
The last time I saw Frank James alive was at the Baltimore Hotel in Kansas City about a year ago. After some casual conversation, he took me aside and said:
"You and I are getting old, and the end may come soon for either of us. There is no man I would prefer to you to say at my funeral such things as your heart may prompt, and if I should go first, I want you to promise to do this for me.
"I so promised, and we are here to fulfill. I was called up last evening by newspaper reporters and asked if I would furnish them a copy of my proposed address. I answered, that I never bury my friends until they are dead. What I shall say here will not be from cold type, but it will be spontaneous, warm from the heart.
"It is a matter of public history that back in the '70s and early part of the '80s, Frank James was a hunted man. I had never met him. Our paths in life had run on divergent lines. He had no other claims on me than the bonds of our common humanity. A mutual friend, Major John N. Edwards, called to see me in 1882 and informed me that Frank James was willing and ready to come in, and surrender to the civil authorities of the State, and desired that I undertake to defend him in court against any charge that had been or might be preferred against him; that all he asked was a fair and impartial hearing, and he was led to believe that I could secure such a trial. He had not a dollar to offer me for such service. It was not in my nature to turn a deaf ear to such an appeal to the spirit of chivalry and charity, no matter what the consequence might be to me personally.
"He did surrender to the Governor of Missouri. At that time, he was under indictment in Jackson County charged

with the crime of train robbery. For reasons satisfactory to those pursuing him, that indictment was abandoned, and another procured in Daviess County, charging him with murder. We met the prosecution upon its chosen field of battle. After a hard-fought contest, in a community and before a tribunal by no means partial to the defendant, he was acquitted. After the excitement of the verdict had measurably subsided Frank forced his way through the crowd, and grasping me by the hand, his wondrous eyes blazing through tears, said:

"I have no words to express to you what my heart feels. I can only say that I can never compensate you for what you have said and done in my behalf."

"I said to him: 'Yes, you can repay me. I have been, as you know, cruelly criticized for my espousal of your defence and expect more of it. But my reward will come when you prove by your future conduct that you are worthy. Take your wife and little boy and make for them a happy home. Acquit yourself like the brave man that you are. Live a clean and honorable life. That will be my compensation.'

"There is no act in my long and varied professional career that has brought me more satisfaction than the feeling that I may have contributed something to give this man his freedom. From that day to this, I followed him with anxious solicitude. He never dissembled with me; but to me wore his heart on his sleeve. I expected he would be pursued by Pharisees who would be delighted should he fall down. I warned him from time to time as we chanced to meet, against the baits and spells of selfish fakirs who would doubtless seek to coin money out of his necessities by tempting him up on the stage in garish shows, exhibiting him before the hungry-eyed rabble as a hero. I conjured him to treat all such tempters as the Saviour did the devil on the mountain.

"With a constitution somewhat shattered, health im-

paired, he was little able to win bread in (sic) the sweat of his face. At times the avenues of compensation, honorable employment, seemed closed against him by a gainsaying world. Now and then the wolf stood at the door. At one time, he attached himself, by contract, to a peripatetic show. It was then that he gave me impressive evidence of his inflexible determination to live honorably, no matter how much poverty might pinch. He called at my chambers, and asked me to examine that contract and advise him how it could be legally avoided; that he had made up his mind, irrevocably, to quit the show, because he had discovered that the ticket seller from the wagon was systematically cheating the patrons, by handing them back, in the bustle about the wagon, less change than they were entitled to receive, with little opportunity, under such conditions, to get back the change that was due them. His decision was to go back to his early love, the farm, where he could eat his bread cankered with no fraud.

"With his little savings, he secured a homestead location in Oklahoma. There he built a cabin, erected the family altar, and pleaded with the mother earth for her bounty, and it came. The visit there of his mother, who had suffered so much of anguish and misfortune because of her unyielding love of her boy "Buck" as she affectionately called Frank, made that rude home a paradise restored to them. On the cars, while returning to her old home, she suddenly died. Then Frank rented out the new-made home, and gathering up his household goods, came back to the old homestead, where its generous soil, that had fed and clothed him in his youth, again yielded its bounty to keep him in peace and plenty. Here he passed the remnant of his life, amid the scenes of his happy boyhood, unvexed in spirit and respected by just men.

"In important respects, Frank James was a man of admirable qualities. Without the adventitious aid of aca-

*demic education, or very inspiring associations, his won-
derful mentality, keen acumen, and thirst for knowledge,
enabled him to absorb such information about men, books
and nature as demonstrated that had opportunity and
dame fortune seconded his gifts, he would have achieved a
brilliant career and honorable fame. From a close observa-
tion of his real character in later life, I feel a positive
conviction that the troublous, tragic life that befell him was
neither of his liking or inclination. He deserved and coveted
better things.*

*"This may not be the time nor the place to extenuate or
condemn the causes that have set down his name in the
colors printed by public opinion. But, as I stood at noon
today on the lawn about the old homestead, just over the hill,
the thought struggled for utterance; what creatures are we
all of circumstances and environments! How often they
shape our destinies, rough hew (sic) them as we may. Sometimes they are factors in forming character itself. As I looked
at the fields, pastures and meadows of that farm, I could,
through the mind's eye, see away back in the fifties a pale
haired, blue-eyed boy, romping, playing, riding and working over them. He was not robust, but wiry, nervous and
intelligent. There was nothing in his conduct to reprobate,
nor was there anything vicious in his temperament. He was
just a plain, simple-hearted farm boy. And I take it he was
rather gentle and tender in his nature, as he was ever the
favored one of his mother, and regarded with affection by
his brothers and sisters. If let alone, to pursue the even tenor
of the way his disposition led, there would have been no
sorrow in the winter of his life.*

*"But he had only passed his majority when the war
clouds spread over the sky above him, which soon broke into
lurid light along the western border of the state. Then like
wolves that come down from the fold, there came out of that
storm bad, lawless men, masquerading in the uniform of*

Frank James in later life. This photograph of him is inscribed, "Uncle Frank, Jerry his dog." Courtesy Ethelrose James.

Union soldiers, who invaded his home, outraging the rights of property and person, turning its peace and happiness into a miniature hell; starting the red blood in the veins of that young man to beating hard and furious, and stirring up the tiger that lay dormant in his heart. Then giving sway to hot passion, booted and spurred, he mounted his horse and rode away, the incarnation of the black spirit of revenge. Like a madman dashing down a blind alley, little reckoning the pitfalls and precipices that might lie at the end, this young man rode on, prodigal in life and heedless of personal danger; until he became infatuated with the glamour of it all. As one false step begets another, he rode on until it seemed fatal to stop and ruin to go forward. But I can say here in the presence of his pulseless face, in the presence of this assembly, that I have reason to believe that all the while the still, small voice of inner conscience never ceased to plead with him for better things; and that if the conservative forces that held his passions in leash could have had their way, and public opinion had sat like mercy alongside of judgment, he, and his more reckless associates, would have been spared the bitter saturnalia of those last years of his hunted life.

"One of the most beautiful things connected with the life of this man was the deep, unaffected affection between him and the gentle woman who sits at my left. Throughout the days and nights of their early wedded life, when the tempests and storms beat so hard upon him, like a good angel she rode and walked by his side, whispering in his ear of peace and hope. Her prayers for his safety and rescue went up unceasingly like the incense from the altar of a pure heart. In the tense strain of the ordeal of that trial at Gallatin, as I pleaded to the jury for the life of Frank James, there was nothing that could have given inspiration to thought and name to tongue so much as the steady, tearful eyes and unblanched cheeks of this brave, devoted woman. With him she went to the new homestead, and with him she came back to the old home. With him she walked and sat beneath those old forest trees, and listened to the wild birds sing. Here she received his parting benediction, and caught the last ray of light in his fading eyes, with that fortitude and serenity that designated her heroic life.

"When at peace with the world, he sought to make his peace with God. His religion was not in tithes or burnt offerings, but of the heart. It was a matter between him and God. Who so mean spirited as to question his sincerity? Who but a publican would wrap himself in the cloak of self-righteousness, and say there is an ascension robe for Frank James? Only the recording angel holds the balance sheet of the wrongs he did and those he suffered, and knows what is written in the Lamb's book.

"The foul spirit of reprobation has lost no opportunity to try and drown the voice of encouragement while Frank was struggling with adversity and temptation, pleading for the passion of compassion and helpfulness. In season and out of season the public press had not failed to print beside

his name, in red letters, the word 'Bandit.' But unmurmuringly he had endured the scoffs and contumely of the mawkish world, as he went on "breast fronted," encouraging duty. Thus he gave irrefragable (sic) proof of his possession of that fortitude and moral courage which enabled Robin Hood, in the closing scene of his tragic life, to show 'mercy for the erring and pity for the weak.'

"Surely the noble in spirit, looking at that face, pallid in death, of this man, can recall and appropriate the words of Shakespeare-the great delineator of human nature-whom Frank James studied as the Mussulman his Koran:

'He that dies pays all debts.'

And there is no generous heart that can resist the impulse of that sympathy and charity— 'one touch of which makes all the world kin'—to utter this sentiment over his bier:

'Oh be his failings covered by the tomb,
May guardian laurels o'er his ashes bloom.'

"My friends: there is something ever depressing about a funeral in the desolateness of winter. The winds moan through these noble trees, bereft of their foliage. The grass on the lawn is withered. The earth lies bleak and chill. The songs of summer birds are hushed and they have gone away. These beautiful flowers which loving hands have laid on this casket will soon lose their fragrance, fade and decay. But we know that after a while the sun will rise higher and higher in the zenith, until its warm rays will melt the ice on the fields, and unlock the streams; that the wild birds will come and sing, as harbingers of spring; the gentle flowers will peep from their wintry beds, and lend their cold cheeks to the genial sun, to be kissed into life and beauty. We know that soon energized life will kindle in the myriad channels of vegetation; and we will again witness the mystery of reproductive growth.

"Thus we have the epitome of the Resurrection—the

assurance that this mortality shall put on immortality. So, whether the dust and ashes of our loved ones mingle with mother earth, or lie in vaults and urns, when the light of the resurrection morn flashes over the world the atoms will be rehabilitated with sentient life and spiritual beauty.

"In this sublime faith, we can see this casket, containing the mortal remains of our friend, borne by friendly hands from this home, with less poignant grief, and with the hope that knows not despair." [56]

Frank's body was taken to St. Louis, Missouri, for cremation by his son, Robert, and his nephew, Jesse James, Jr. Robert's mother had asked him to remain with his father's body at all times.

Robert told his mother they would ride in the baggage car with the body. If he could not stay awake, he would sleep on top of the coffin.

Robert had all the metal taken off the coffin. [57] This he carried with him and dropped into the Missouri River as the train crossed over the bridge on the return trip home. Frank's ashes were placed in a vault in a Kansas City bank (New England Safe Deposit Co. and the Kearney Trust Co.) until the death of his wife, Anna, when they were then buried in a grave with hers in a private cemetery at Independence, Missouri, not far from the Rock Creek School House where Anna had taught school before she married Frank James. [58]

[56] *Kansas City Star,* March 28th, 1915

[57] The metal was taken off the coffin before it was cremated.

[58] Frank and Anna are buried in Hill Cemetery, now a part of Jackson County, Hill Park, Independence, Missouri. His name on the marker is "Alexander F. James." Annie (called Anna) Ralston James died aged 91, on July 6th, 1944 at Excelsior Springs, Missouri. Her body was also cremated.

While Jesse and Robert were taking Frank James's body to St. Louis, I remained, with our four daughters, at the farm, to be of what help I could.

Just before the funeral, Estelle, our third daughter, had become very ill. As soon as possible, that same afternoon, right after the funeral, a doctor was called, and he arrived shortly after Jesse, Jr. and Robert, had departed.

The doctor examined Estelle and informed me that we had a very bad case of diphtheria. He ordered all the anti-toxin that was in Kearney to be sent at once, and he remained with our sick daughter all through the night.

The next morning, a second daughter was ill, and we were told that she, too, had diphtheria. A call was made to the wholesale drug companies of Kansas City to send in a large supply of anti-toxin, by the first train coming to Kearney.

During the following day, the other two girls came down with diphtheria. Dr. Bailey was a young doctor, and new in Kearney; but we were to learn that he was a very good one-and a very busy one. In the next few weeks, there were more than a dozen cases of diphtheria in Kearney and in the county. We were under quarantine for five weeks in bitter winter weather.

When Jesse returned from St. Louis and had word of our plight, he brought our family doctor over from the city. Dr. Alexander did what he could, but assured us that Dr. Bailey was doing a splendid job.

Later, Dr. Alexander informed us that one of my nieces, who had spent the night with us after recovering from diphtheria, had been examined and found to be the carrier of the disease. She had exposed all of our girls at the same time. Many cases developed in the school she attended, and that school was closed, as were other schools in and around Kearney.

Fortunately, there were no deaths as a result of the

epidemic. But we will never forget our trip to Uncle Frank's funeral and our prolonged stay on the farm, or the many sleepless nights and even busier days. [59] Robert James and his wife, Mae, who were living on the farm at that time, were wonderful. So was Mae's brother Joe Sanboth, who was spending the winter with them. Joe became our "outside-chambermaid." He made dozens of trips during the day and night, through the snow. When he was not going to the little house in the garden, he was piling wood outside. Robert kept the fire going day and night.

It was Robert who met the postman each day, to get food that was sent in by neighbors and relatives. The snow was knee deep, and Robert had to be at the road when the mail-carrier arrived. If he had not been there, the baked ham, bread and cooked chicken would have been carried away by hungry dogs, or else frozen to the ground.

I think Robert and Joe slept in their boots. Our only callers were Dr. Bailey and Jesse, when he could get away from the office. Jesse had to come out by horseback, because of the deep snow. One day, he arrived on foot! He had lost the horse, or as he put it, "the horse had lost him." He had come through the pasture where the snowdrifts were so deep the horse could not get through. So, off went Robert and Joe, to the rescue!

If it had not been for Robert's jolly nature, our stay would have been much more distressing. He and his sweet wife, Mae, and Joe were all three kind to us, and unfailingly cheerful.

But, as we were leaving the farm, I suspect that Robert expressed an honest feeling when he pointed to the sign on the gate that read: "Kodaks Barred"–and told the girls he was going to change the sign to read "Relatives Barred!"

[59] On a visit to the James Farm Historic Site in 1987, Ethel Rose (she uses this spelling) vividly remembered having spent those weeks with her mother and sisters in the south parlor of the little house.

FAMILY LIFE

During the early years of our marriage, Jesse's business prospered. His cigar and tobacco store in the Junction Building, at 9th, Main and Delaware Streets,[60] continued to flourish as time went on, soon reaching the point where he could hire help to take over in the evenings, freeing him to pursue his original ambition: to study law.[61]

Jesse graduated from the Kansas City School of Law on June 5th, 1907. It was a happy day for our family. An item in the *St. Louis Dispatch* reflected some of our own sense of triumphant achievement:

"A youth who is carving out an honorable career, despite the handicap of a bad name, makes another step up.

"Jesse James, the son of Jesse James the Missouri outlaw, is now a full fledged lawyer. Last week he passed a successful examination before the State Board of Examiners. In a class of 37, Jesse James stood first.

"His average in all branches was 91 per cent. Henry Ashly, Chairman of the Board of Examiners, said after the examination that Jesse James was the brightest legal mind

---

[60] One of his customers was another young man of promise in Kansas City; Harry S. Truman. Please see appendix.

[61] From 1902-1906, Jesse, Jr. is listed in the Kansas City directories as operating the "Jesse James Collateral Loan Company" at 1215 1/2, Grand Ave.

Mr. and Mrs. Jesse James, Jr. Courtesy Ethelrose James.

of any young man who had ever appeared before the board. "Jesse is a self-made man. He was handicapped as few boys are. His father was killed when he was six years old. Without money, and with the heritage of a bad name, he nevertheless persevered in the honorable course he had chosen."

Now Jesse sold his business and embarked upon a career as an attorney in Kansas City. He loved his practice, and put in long hours, working even harder than he had during the years when he had managed to combine his studies with the necessity of earning a good living for his family.[62]

But he still found time to spend with his children and me. Jesse, Jr. was a kind and loving father, but not a wise one in all matters. He would shower affection on his daughters, but he was entirely too lenient when it came to discipline.

In his opinion, children should not be spanked. I am sure that he never in his life struck one of his children. If they needed to be spanked, it had to be done when their father was not around.

When Ethelrose was three, I spanked her one evening and put her on a chair in the kitchen while I was preparing dinner. She soon forgot her hurt feelings until she heard her father come in.

Then she wanted sympathy and started to cry, saying, "Mommie spanked me!"

I told her to tell her father why I had spanked her.

She thought for a moment, and then said, "Because you're the biggest!"

The only bloodshed that I recall occurring in our family due to our kinship with Jesse James happened when

---

[62] Jesse was 32 years old when he graduated with honors from Kansas City School of Law, and received his diploma on the stage of the Shubert Theatre on June 5th, 1907. Please see appendix.

our Jo Frances was about four years old. She was playing in our yard. The neighborhood children would come in to play in the sand pile. One of them named Bobbie had a bad habit of throwing sand on the other children, and I had told him that he would be sent home if he kept throwing sand.

Jo came in one day to tell me that Bobbie had put sand in her hair. I went out and told him to go home and to tell his mother just why he had been banished.

A few minutes later, I could hear Bobbie calling from the yard something about Jesse James being a train robber. Jo came stomping in and demanded: "Come out and tell Bobbie that my daddy is a lawyer!"

She was told to pay no attention to him, that he was just angry.

In a few minutes I heard Bobbie screaming as if he were being killed. When I hurried out, I could not believe my eyes. Jo was coming home with her little shovel in her hand. Bobbie's mother was wiping blood from his face.

I was in the act of picking my vicious little daughter up for a sound spanking, when she looked at me and said, "Pay no attention—I was just mad!"

She was to learn that day that she could not defend the name of Jesse James with a shovel in her hand. Jo had heard of only one Jesse James, and that was the gentle, doting father she adored.

I remember one Christmas when our children were small. There was a dreadful blizzard that demolished transportation. Jesse strapped a box of toys and gifts onto a large sled and walked about three miles to deliver them to our colored laundress and her children on Christmas Eve.

Another time, when he defended the son of a widow on a very serious charge, the woman did not have any money. She told Jesse that if he would defend her son, she would have to give him the deed to her house. After the boy was acquitted, and the mother rushed over to thank Jesse, he took the deed from his briefcase and handed it back to her, saying he had just paid a debt of gratitude.

Long hours of hard work eventually took their toll, and in 1926 Jesse, Jr., suffered a decline in health which forced him into semi-retirement.

He and the girls and I came to California in the fall of that year, expecting only to spend the winter. Then, as Jesse's health improved to the point where he wanted to take up his practice again, he decided he liked California and would remain, opening a law office in Los Angeles.

CHAPTER 13

LAST
TRAGEDY

We made new friends in California, and in many ways it was a new and different way of life for us. People whom we eventually came to know well, when they became aware of our Missouri background sometimes asked us if being grandchildren of Jesse James was ever a handicap or source of embarrassment for our four daughters. I cannot recall that this had been a handicap. We never advertised that we were of the Jesse James family, nor did we ever make an effort to conceal the fact. We were acquainted with many people for years before they ever came to know of the family connection.

There were some humorous incidents because of this. Once for example, at our daughter Estelle's club meeting, the theme, or topic of discussion was "Our Pioneer Ancestors." During the luncheon, each member was to tell of an interesting ancestor.

The president of the club was a charming and dignified person. She began by saying that her Uncle Willie had ridden with Jesse James. She then gave a talk on Jesse's and Willie's histories.

Later, when Estelle was to speak, her subject being Daniel Boone, she started by saying that she "did not want to steal Madame president's thunder," but her grandfather not only rode with Jesse James, "he was Jesse James!"

There was a roar of laughter, but no one believed Estelle until someone looked at me and exclaimed, "Your name is James! Can Estelle's story be true?"

Estelle had been in the club for a number of years, but, as she was married, she had never been known as Estelle James.

Our youngest daughter had been employed by the Federal Reserve Bank for a number of years, when one of the fake "Jesse Jameses" went to the bank and announced that he was Jesse James, and that he understood that his granddaughter, Ethelrose James, worked there, and he wanted to see her!

The guard sent word to the personnel director, who called Ethelrose into his office. The bank official thought the old man was crazy, and he asked Ethelrose why he should pick on her.

She told him it must be because she was the grand-daughter of Jesse James.

The bank official looked at Ethelrose for a moment, shook his head, and said, "Jesse James' granddaughter, working with millions all around her! Well, I'll be damned."

Ethelrose had worked as secretary in various departments of the bank, including the money counting department. She continued to work at the bank until she left to be married. [63] It was such amusing incidents which were apt to come to mind when people asked me if the notoriety of my husband's father had ever created difficulties for our daughters.

The truth, however, is that there have been some tragic incidents, too.

While Jo Frances was a freshman at the University of Missouri, she wrote to tell her father how happy she was at being invited to join one of the sororities there. But time passed, and she did not become a member. Eventually we

[63] According to Ethelrose, the bank guards made the incident even more amusing by "covering" the bogus "outlaw" with their guns, while he waited for the arrival of his "granddaughter."

learned that she had been heart-broken to find that she was being black-balled because she was the grand-daughter of Jesse James.

Jo·did not return to the University after her first year. She later married a young man who had gone through grade and high school with her. He was the son of an Army Colonel, whose wife was not pleased with the idea of her son being married to the granddaughter of Jesse James.

After the birth of a son, this marriage was not a happy one, and terminated in divorce. Jo Frances brought her little son home to live with Jesse and me.

The little boy was a gift from heaven in our home. We had not been blessed with a son of our own. The relationship between "Sonny Jim" and his grandfather was like that of father and son. [64]

For Jesse, Jr., himself, the most distressing consequence of his father's notoriety had been his false arrest, on the charge of train robbery, in 1898, the year before I met him. But that was not to be the end of his sorrows. I think the last great tragedy in the life of Jesse James, Jr., was in 1920, when he entered into contract to play the role of his father in a motion picture. The name of the picture was *Jesse James Under the Black Flag.* The picture was made by Mesco Picture Company, with offices in Kansas City. It was an independent company, incorporated: A large number of Jesse, Jr.'s friends and relatives bought stock in the company and many of his business acquaintances invested.

---

[64] Jo Frances James married Ronald Ross on September 2nd, 1925. Their child is (1989) California Superior Court Judge James Randall Ross. It was "Joey" who worked on the script of the1939 Twentieth Century Fox movie, *Jesse James,* starring Tyrone Power and Henry Fonda. Although given a prominent credit in the opening frames of the movie, the final script owed little to Joey's material, and bore only a slight resemblance to the truth. On moving to California, Jo Frances James became a close friend of the silent movie star, William S. Hart.

The James family on the lawn of the Clinton County Court house, Plattsburg, Missouri, during the filming of the movie Jessie James Under the Black Flag *in 1920. Jesse James, Jr. in costume as his father, is in the center of the back row. Stella James is on his left, as are Norma and John Samuel, half-brother of Jesse James. Mary, Jesse, Jr.'s sister, stands to his right, and to her right are Effie Nicholson, Belle Nicholson and "Uncle Joe" Hall, brother-in-law of Jesse. On the second row, L-R, are: Harry Nicholson, Addie Hall, Arch Nicholson, George Hall, Frank Nicholson and Leda Nicholson. On the front row are: Nadine Nicholson, Perry Samuel, Josephine Hall and John Nicholson. James Farm Collection.*

I knew the idea of playing the part of his father in this picture was distasteful to Jesse from the beginning. He had, from the time he was a very young man, refused many offers of high pay to exhibit himself on the stage in some sensational play or other lurid manner, choosing instead to work very hard for a livelihood for his mother and sister.

But the Mesco Company made Jesse a very tempting offer, running into five figures. Jesse was ambitious. He had four daughters to put through college, so that they might enjoy the advantages he had never had.

His mother was dead now. His Uncle Frank had passed on, too. His sister Mary was happily married, with three fine sons. It seemed to Jesse, Jr, that no one would be hurt by his participation in a portrayal of his father's life now. And he was convinced, too, that the script which Mesco Company had showed him offered an honest, if not especially artistic, delineation of the James story.

He talked the matter over with me at length, before arriving at his decision. On the one hand, there was the fact that he was, at the time, a successful attorney with a good practice, a nice home, and four lovely daughters. On the other hand, with two of his daughters in high school and one already attending the University of Missouri, he had use for added income; and many of his friends, relatives and business associates had confidence in the Mesco Company.

So at last he agreed to make *Jesse James Under the Black Flag* and *Jesse James the Outlaw*. What this decision was ultimately to cost him, in peace of mind and eventually broken health, neither of us could foresee.

The director and camera man came from New York. The cast consisted largely of amateurs and very poor actors, Jesse being the worst of the lot. I was told that he fainted twice during the filming of the scene depicting the killing of his father.

The pictures were completed in a studio in Chicago, but not before the money had expired. In order to save the stockholder's investments, more money had to be raised. Jesse felt largely responsible for the investments of his friends and relatives. He felt that they might have been influenced by his connection with the pictures. Our home was mortgaged, as were the homes and farms of some of the company management.

When the pictures were finished, Jesse travelled through the East, on tour with the show, for four months. Being an independent production, they had to be exhibited as a road

The re-enactment of the raid by the James-Younger Gang on the First National Bank of Northfield, Minnesota, staged for the 1921 movie, Jesse James the Outlaw. *Courtesy R. Roberts.*

show. They were a complete failure and a financial loss.[65]

Jesse returned to his home in Kansas City, heartbroken and sick. He was not able to return to his law practice for more than a year. When he did return to his practice for a short time, he suffered a nervous collapse.

The family had moved into an apartment when our house was sold. Now Jesse left us to spend months in a hospital. By the time he was well enough to come home, we had moved again, to a large house near Independence, Missouri. Our daughters had finished high school and left college. They all took jobs.

It was in October of 1926 that Jesse and I with our youngest daughter came to California, where Jesse recov-

[65] Please see appendix.

ered his health sufficiently to open a law office in Los Angeles.

So, when people asked if our kinship with Jesse James had ever been a handicap for our daughters, I usually replied quite truthfully that it had not, that indeed, the occasional incident arising from this kinship was more likely than not to be humorous.

But I cannot deny that the shadow of the past made itself felt in my husband's life, more than once. And, though he was able to resume his law practice in California for two years, Jesse James, Jr., was a sick man until he passed away on March 26th, 1951.[66]

---

[66] Jesse James, Jr. is buried in Forest Lawn Memorial Park, Glendale, California.

CHAPTER 14

THE SHADOW

The past which had cast its shadow on Jesse, Jr.'s life was to linger over the lives of his family after his death.

An old man, driving two thin horses hitched to a covered wagon, arrived in Excelsior Springs, Missouri, one autumn day in 1931.

He paused in his wanderings to camp in a wooded spot near a small stream of water, at the edge of town. He spent most of his time, in the days that followed, sitting around the combination Police and Fire Station, chatting with other old men.

When it was learned that his name was John James, he was told many stories about Frank and Jesse James. Some of these old men had known the James family, and others had known Frank and Jesse as boys. Still others told of the times the James boys had stayed a night in their home, or in the homes of their families, when they would come to see their mother.

John James was told how "Aunt Margaret," an old resident of Excelsior Springs, who was blind, had been a girl friend of Jesse James, and how she would carry messages to Jesse's mother, and would take food to the James boys when they would be in hiding.

He also heard of the times when the James boys would have a close call with the law-enforcement agents who pursued them but never quite caught up with them.

John James did more listening than talking.

John James emerged as the outlaw Jesse James in 1932 at Excelsior Springs, Missouri, close to the old James Farm. Claiming that another outlaw, Charlie Bigelow had been killed in his stead, he enjoyed brief celebrity until he was exposed by Stella James and his true identity revealed. Committed to an asylum by his sister, he died there in 1947.

He decided to visit "Aunt Margaret." He repeated to her some of the stories he had heard.

Aunt Margaret asked him how he knew about these things, as some of them were known only to herself and Jesse.

It was at this moment that John James became "Jesse James." He said he had come home in his old age to see some of his old friends. Blind and aged, "Aunt Margaret" believed him

John James had made this same claim many times as a young man, in his wanderings over the countryside of Iowa and Illinois as a horse trader. But he had never made the claim to anyone so willing to believe him.

John James was put up in the best hotel in Excelsior Springs, to live in luxury. His horses were housed in the livery stable. They, too, were well kept.

His story made headlines in Los Angeles, as well as in most of the other big cities of the nation. Jesse, Jr., and I, had been receiving letters from an unknown man in Excelsior Springs asking questions about Jesse's mother, the widow of Jesse James, and other members of the family. We had disregarded these letters, and we were not disturbed about the old man's claims, as there had been a number of others in years gone by.

Then a reporter from a Los Angeles newspaper called on us. He had been to Excelsior Springs to interview the old man. He told us that he had had to do most of his talking to the old man's promoter. He said that some of the city officials were backing this latest imposter.

Jesse, Jr., was ill at the time. Now he became disturbed to the extent that he felt he must find out who was behind the scheme and why. He thought it must be a publicity stunt for a movie.

When a Los Angeles newspaper suggested that I go back to Excelsior Springs and give the old man a public hearing, I decided to do just that. I found that Bill Payne, the local Chief of Police, was in charge of the promotion. He had taken affidavits from six or seven of the old-timers who were quite sure that the man was Jesse James, as well as one from "Aunt Margaret."

The hearing was held with men from the press, and the James kin present, none of whom had ever been contacted about the identity of this man.

The hearing was a mockery. The old man was a pathetic figure. He had been coached as to the names and ages of the James family. His "Textbook" was the book that had been written by Jesse, Jr., in 1899, in which the family history had been printed.

Even with this help, the old man could not answer all of the questions that were put to him. He did not know the name or the age of the little child, Archie Peyton Samuel, who was killed at the time the explosive was thrown into the house, nor did he know which arm Mrs. Samuel had lost.[67]

The woman who was acting as secretary to John James was an intelligent person, who could recognize the absurdity of it all. She was a great help to me.

She had learned that John James was on parole from the penitentiary in Southern Illinois, where he had been serving time for killing a man. She wrote for the family history of John James, given at the time he entered the penitentiary.

A visit was made to the old home town of John James's family, and all the living members were traced. A sister, Doctor Bessie James Garver, was living in Los Angeles I learned.

After returning home, I called on Dr. Garver. She told me that she had read the newspaper stories about the man

---

[67] Please see appendix.

in Excelsior Springs, and she believed him to be her brother. Dr. Bessie Garver volunteered to go to the office of an attorney and give an affidavit about her brother, John James, and other members of her family.

We had hoped that the matter had been disposed of after the hearing in Excelsior Springs and the exposé of the promoter. We were wrong, for John James came to Los Angeles. He was armed with his affidavits and a new promoter. He made radio broadcasts, and appeared at one of the beaches as a paid attraction.

He came to our house and demanded to see Jesse James, Jr. He was not admitted. He also went to the bank where our daughter, Ethelrose was employed, and asked to see her, claiming to be her grandfather.

At this point I readily agreed to Dr. Garver's offer of an affidavit establishing the facts about her brother's identity, and this she did before Charles R. Thompson, later a Judge of the superior Court of California.

Dr. Garver stated that her brother was "not possessed of a normal mind." She went on to say, "I make this affidavit for the purpose of having said William John James, my brother, committed to the proper institution for the insane, verily believing that such course is to the best interest of my brother, and to society, feeling that, as a physician, his disease is progressing and that he might become dangerous to society."

John James died in the State Hospital for the Mentally Ill at Little Rock, Arkansas, on December 24th, 1947.

A year and a half after John James's death, a new Jesse James was brought out with fanfare by two reporters in Lawton, Oklahoma, and this man came to Los Angeles with new promoters, but with the same affidavits that John James had obtained in Excelsior Springs!

This old man was Frank Dalton. He was an invalid, and was moved to and from airplanes on a stretcher, and in an

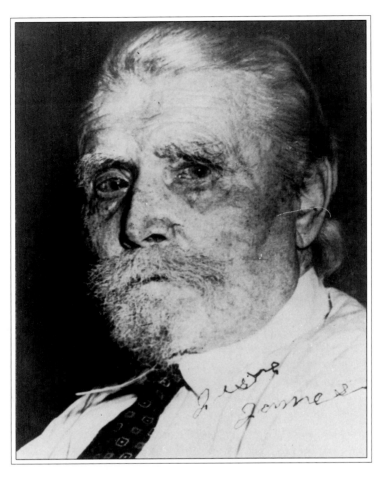

*J. Frank Dalton. Described by an authority as a "splendid
cosmic charlatan ... he reeks of snake oil, shell games and
sawdust" (Steve Eng in Ted Yeatman's* Study of Spurious James
Works, Show Me Libraries, *May 1983, page 32), J. Frank
Dalton insisted he was the outlaw Jesse James, despite the
strenuous denials of the James family and legitimate historians. Larger physically than the real Jesse, he lacked the bullet
wounds to the chest and hand the outlaw was known to have
suffered. (Interview with his nurse, the former Mrs. Orvus Lee
Howk, December, 1989).*

ambulance, and with a nurse. This outfit gained some publicity by giving out a false story that Jesse, Jr., was going to visit his old father. The public was invited to visit the old man and hear his amazing story. I did go out to see him—incognito, of course, as I was interested in seeing the affidavits. They were the same ones I had seen in Excelsior Springs, declaring that John James was Jesse James...I had talked to each of the old people that had given them.[68]

I will go no further into the claim of Frank Dalton, except to reprint parts of two articles that *he* sent to Huston H. Crittenden for publication in the *"Crittenden Memoirs* in 1936 (pages 364 and 368). These are in the chapter entitled, "My Adventures with Jesse James;"

"Of course, Jesse has been seen alive from time to time by cheap notoriety seekers. Once a cowboy came up from the Argentine and said that Jesse was ranching and doing well down there. When this report was sifted down, it was found that the man taken for Jesse was the younger son of an English Lord.

"A few years ago, a banker in a West Texas town died, and a report was spread that he was Jesse James. More recently a fellow popped up claiming to be Jesse! How the heck do they get that way, loco weed, or what?

"No! Jesse James was killed by Bob Ford on the 3rd of April, 1882. In St. Joseph, Missouri, there were too many people who knew him well and came to identify him for there to be any possible doubt, so that is that."

[68] The Lawton, Oklahoma, *Constitution*, showing incredible gullibility, announced with bold headlines in its May 19th, 1948 edition that "JESSE JAMES IS ALIVE IN LAWTON" claiming the real Jesse James had not been killed in St. Joseph, Missouri on April 3rd, 1882. Please see appendix.

105

&

"I was in Fort Riley, Kan. (sic), when Bob Ford shot him on April 3rd, 1882, and it was known that I soldiered with him under Quantrell during the latter part of the Civil War. I was sent for to identify him and did so to the best of my ability and have always been positive (am yet for that matter) that the man killed by Ford was Jesse James.

&

If you wonder why I have given space to these last two in a series of pretenders to the name of Jesse James, and the last pretenders they will be, as Jesse James would be 115 years old by now, it is because a new crop of imposters is being forced upon the public now, in the guise of Jesse James, Jr., and Jesse James the Third.[69]

A motion picture company in Hollywood made a picture, which was shown on television, featuring the man who claimed to be "Jesse James the Third". I have a letter from one of the producers of the television show in which he stated that he knew the man claiming to be "Jesse James the Third" was a liar and an imposter; but that they would put the story on the air anyway!

It seems that if you die in California, you do not have a right to privacy. That is, your living relatives do not have a right to privacy. The moral to this is, if your name is James, just don't die in California. It is a nice place to live in, but when it comes time to die, just move on to a state where you can die and your family would have a right of privacy.

---

[69] Orvus Lee Howk, a wildcat oil man and showman claimed that he was Jesse James' (AKA J. Frank Dalton's) grandson "Jesse Lee James III," (there seems never to have been a Jesse Lee James I and II). Please see appendix.

And remember, if you ever see a movie about Stella James, who is portrayed as a "so-and so," I won't be here to deny it. So, I am telling you now, "'T'ain't so!"

It is because of such impositions as these that I have elevated these two preposterous examples of Jesse James 'pretenders' to a place of any importance of this story.

And so the shadow of the past lingers on. It was with mixed emotions, one afternoon in April, 1958, that my four daughters and two of my grandchildren and I threaded our way through Hollywood in a caravan of three cars, to one of the major studios, to preview yet another motion picture. This picture had been announced on a television program known as "Playhouse 90" the night before as the coming attraction to be shown the following week. The name of the picture was "Bitter Heritage," portraying a segment of the life of the real Jesse James, Jr., the son of Jesse James the Missouri outlaw, my husband.

All of us in this caravan were shocked, hurt and confused. We had always believed that Jesse James, Jr., had been a private citizen with some right of privacy. We could not understand how this picture could have been made without the knowledge and permission of the widow and family of Jesse James, Jr., who had passed away just seven years previously, following a long illness.

My Grandson, James Ross, then a practicing attorney in Los Angeles, was concerned primarily with the legal situation, as were the attorneys accompanying him; while my granddaughter was apprehensive about the portrayal of her grandfather and anxious to learn what sort of actor had been given the role.

My daughters were sad, but thankful that their father could not know about this picture.

As for myself, I was trembling with apprehension. Would this picture be another spectacle of violence and gun play, as the other Jesse James films had been? If so, could I sit through it?

It was. And I did sit through it.

Young Jesse was shown in the picture riding back to the farm home of his grandmother with Frank James, after an absence of some fifteen years, wondering how they would be received by the townspeople. The picture portrayed the sheriff warning them that they were not wanted in Kearney, and advising them to leave.

I was remembering that Jesse, Jr., had spent his boyhood in Kansas City, Missouri, very near his grandmother's farm. I could vividly recall his telling me how, as a boy, he would visit his grandmother and go fishing and hunting in the quiet countryside.

I also remembered how, during the early years of our marriage, he would sit over his law books, studying far into the night, and then rise early to go into town to tend his cigar store during the day.

I remembered, too, how young Jesse enjoyed taking his family for a visit to his grandmother's home, sitting under the big coffee bean tree that sheltered the grave of his father. I remembered how, later, we'd all enjoy visiting Uncle Frank James and his devoted wife, Anna, when they were living in their neat cottage on that same farm.

Grandma Samuel and Uncle Frank had both been so proud of young Jesse when he had graduated from law college with the highest honors in his class of thirty-eight and passed the bar examination with the highest grade.

As these memories of what actually happened went through my mind, what I was seeing on the screen was such an obvious distortion of the facts that I could not even think of it as an insult to my dead husband's memory, for there seemed no possible connection between this caricature and the wonderful man who had been such a fine citizen, such a devoted husband and father, all through our more than fifty years together.

Now as the shooting in the picture died down, my own thoughts were far removed from its ugly lies, for I was lost in reminiscences of the good life we had shared until my Jesse was laid to rest in the beautiful Forest Lawn Memorial Park, on a slope overlooking a green valley.

When the picture was over, I told my attorney grandson, "I will leave the outcome in your hands and the judgment of the courts of our State. Now I would just like to drive out to Forest lawn, and try to forget what I have just seen."[70]

The shadow of the past is with us still. But although it sometimes darkened our lives, it cannot tarnish my memories. Nor can it ever change the truth.

The legend, with all its distortions, may persist. But I am content if my own account of the part of the legend serves to make the public a little more aware of the truth.

THE END

‏‮‬

---

[70] Please see appendix.

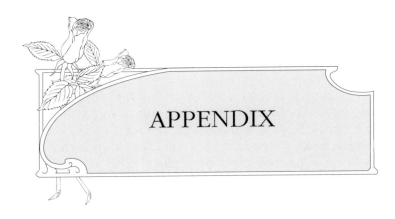

APPENDIX

6. Neither Jesse, Jr. nor Stella were aware of the details or significance of the residency of Jesse James and his family in Kansas City during the summer of 1881. For the first time, here is information about his life-style there and information on some surprisingly bungled train robberies, indicating that perhaps Jesse was not always the master planner that he was thought to have been. Young Jesse remembered only that he could not play with neighborhood children as often as he wanted. He could not realize how daring this period was, Jesse living in the city where he was probably better known than anywhere else, planning and committing robberies there, freely strolling the streets and wearing no disguise, as if he was challenging the authorities.

Both he and his wife, Zee, were familiar with this city of 80,000. She had grown up there and he on a farm only twenty-five miles away. They had a number of relatives there (Jesse and his wife were, of course, first cousins); among them, Thomas M. James, an uncle, who owned a successful china importing business, a pillar of the community; Rev. William James, another uncle who had married them; and her sisters and brother. In fact they had lived there in 1875.

Frank James was equally at home there, and his wife, Annie Ralston, had grown up in Independence, just to the east.

In 1872 Jesse, Frank and one of the Younger brothers held up the box office of the Kansas City Exposition in a daring daylight robbery and, in 1879, the gang committed the famous Glendale robbery near Independence.

Both had been living in Nashville, Tennessee for several years. They left hurriedly in late March, 1881 after reading in the newspapers of the capture of Bill Ryan, a member of the gang. They went, first to the home of their uncle, George Hite in Kentucky and then to see an old friend and former "associate," Donny Pence, then, amazingly, the Sheriff of Nelson County.

Here, they made plans to return to Kansas City, not only to live but to continue train robbery. In Nashville, both worked; they discarded this pretension in Kansas City. Jesse had learned from newspapers that the Missouri River was flooding there and on April 23rd an engine of the Hannibal & St. Joseph Railroad fell into the water north of the city. Traffic was suspended and passengers taken to Kansas City from the north by boat from Randolph, four miles downstream. Here, Jesse planned to rob the New York-Kansas City express which was due to arrive at 9:07 p.m. as passengers were being transferred.

To allay possible suspicion, Jesse went north from Kentucky and rode the Hannibal to Kearney, Missouri, near his mother's farm. There, he met Frank, who had come through St. Louis. Zee and their children arrived in Kansas City on May 1st, accompanied by their cousin, Clarence Hite. Frank's wife and son stopped at the home of Confederate General Jo Shelby for several days before going to her father's in Independence. Zee, young Jesse and Mary stayed with her sister, Mrs. Charles McBride.

On May 4th, the river subsided enough for trains to cross the bridge, and the robbery was, therefore, cancelled. Jesse and Frank joined their wives.

As "J.T. Jackson," Jesse moved to the Doggett House at Sixth and Walnut, telling young Jesse they were moving to another city. A week later while he was playing in front of the hotel he saw McBride pass by.

"Hello, Uncle Charlie," he called, "How did you get to this town?"

McBride hastily acknowledged the boy and rode off. When Jesse was told he, "at once paid the bill and moved." (The flight from Tennessee, robbery plans and arrivals in Missouri are mentioned in the confessions of Dick Liddle and Clarence Hite in Geo. Miller, Comp., *The Trial of Frank James for Murder* (Kansas City,1898) 36-38; 50-51; 307, hereafter: *Trial.* Accounts of the flood are in the Kansas City newspapers, esp. the *Journal,* April 2lst-May 4th, 1881. See also *Jesse James Jr., 7.*)

The house on Woodland Avenue was rented on June 1st from D.R. Abeel, a former newspaperman. They moved in with newly-purchased furniture, "new but poor," both paid with from the $1,700 that was Jesse's share of the robbery of a government payroll messenger near Muscle Shoals, Alabama on March 11th, 1881. It was a structure on the east side of the street about midway between Eleventh and Twelfth Streets, just east of the city limits. Next door, across a thirty foot vacant lot lived John, father of Cornelius Murphy, the Marshal of Jackson County.

Jesse rarely kept a horse in Kansas City and walked extensively. Groceries and meat were delivered.

"Kansas City was the safest place we could get," Zee said, "for people would not suspect us of living here." Jesse went all over town. "He wore no disguise."

Neighbors thought Mr. Jackson was a gambler "as he seemed to do no work." Once he was away for two weeks at the time of the Winston train robbery. His wife said he had "gone to some springs for his health." He was a quiet, "crabbed," rather sour-tempered man they thought, who made it plain he did not want company between his many comings and goings. Actually this was the opposite of his true nature. On the other hand, Zee was a "very kindly disposed and neighborly woman" who once helped lay out the corpse of a neighbor's child and make funeral arrangements.

Little Jesse did play with a few children and one boy got into a fight with him and threw a stone, which hit "Mr. Jackson" who had come to break it up. And another boy, Harry Hoffman, became a life-long friend. *Kansas City Journal* April 4, 5, 6, 13th, 1882; *Star*, April 21st, 1882; *Trial*, 314, *Jesse James Jr.*, 7. Hoffman, James Farm Collection.

Once the families were settled, Jesse began planning another robbery. He met the others at his mother's farm several times in June.

"He told me after one trip," reported Zee, "that he had gotten on the train at the (Kansas City) bridge depot. When the conductor came along (collecting tickets) he noticed he had (a joint of) one finger off. Upon his coming back Jesse said (the same conductor) stopped him and asked if he was Jesse James, telling him that Jesse was minus such a joint." *Kansas City Journal*, April 13th, 1882.

Another example of Jesse's boldness while living in Kansas City was reported by a friend.

"One night in October '81, I was walking up Twelfth Street, Kansas City and on the corner of Oak I met Jesse. He was not disguised at all. We walked together down Twelfth to Main, passing on the corner of Grand Avenue. Officers (Tillman) Crabtree and (Henry C.) Nichols (evidently acquaintances). Hailing a hack, we entered it, and proceeded to take in the town."

They saw a performance from a private box at the Coliseum Theatre, visited several restaurants and saloons. At one, a patron, seeing the sombrero Jesse wore, called out "Gentlemen, this is Jesse James in disguise" while the piano player sang a bit of doggerel about Jesse.

"Jesse's face flushed slightly with anger, but he good-humouredly set 'em up ...." Anon. *The Life and Tragic*

Death of Jesse James, (1882). Reprint, (Austin, TX, 1966); 23.
They decided to rob a train of the Chicago, Rock Island
& Pacific Railroad near Chillicothe, in northern Missouri,
and four men, Jesse, Frank, Wood Hite and Liddle rode
there. By the time they arrived, June 8th, a heavy rain had
made the roads nearly impassable and the plan was
cancelled.

They set out again about June 12th. Near Gallatin, an
abscessed tooth caused Jesse such great pain and swelling
he was put aboard a train at Hamilton and taken back to
Kansas City.

On Independence Day, Jesse walked to the depot,
pausing to read bulletins on the condition of President
James A. Garfield who had been shot. ("HE LIVES" they
screamed.) The group assembled near Gallatin again on July
14th, but miscalculated, and the train passed by before they
could stop it. The next night, they took no chances and
boarded a train at the Winston station.

When the Rock Island train from Kansas City pulled
out of the depot at 11 p.m., five men jumped aboard. The
safe was robbed and the train stopped a mile down the track
where they had tied their horses. During the robbery one of
the men, probably Jesse, shot and killed the conductor and
a passenger, perhaps by accident.

They fled south, riding all night, reaching the Crooked
River country at dawn, where the money was equally
divided. They were severely disappointed, each receiving
only $130. Here, they split; Jesse, Frank and Clarence Hite
going into the town of Lawson, where they had supper with
a farm woman. Later, they rode towards the James Farm,
boldly greeting several persons along the way. They slept in
the woods about three miles from the farm, then camped in
a grove of trees behind the house. There, Mrs. Samuel, John
Samuel, and Will Nicholson, Jesse's favorite brother-in-law,
brought them food. Jesse returned home Sunday. Details of

the escape from Winston are found in *Trial*, 312-313.

To ride to that location was a most audacious act, for at the very same time, Clay County Sheriff James R. Timberlake was "scouring" the same area with his posse. Indeed, they approached the Samuel residence early Sunday, July 17th, while the outlaws were resting nearby! Perhaps they passed too early, for Timberlake had gone in Kearney so he could take a 7:00 am train. Even though he "knew every inch of the territory" his timing was poor.

Meanwhile reports (that were quite accurate) that Frank and Jesse had been seen in Kansas City and at their mother's appeared in the press. They had been tracked to Lawson and, by Sunday the escape route was known.

Mrs. Samuel made an appearance in Kearney on Monday and was seen returning from Kansas City the next day. Whom she visited is not known. She denied her sons had committed a robbery and claimed they were both dead.

Jesse was safe at home on Woodland Avenue. Here, on Monday morning he was roused by a commotion in the vacant lot. He discovered Marshal Murphy had chosen the spot to form a posse to find the outlaws. Seeing "Mr. Jackson," Murphy invited him to join in, feeling he could get "dozens of determined men." "Jackson," of course declined the offer. This was probably the incident handed down to Jesse, Jr.

Kansas City Times July 17, 18, 19, 20th., 1881; *Kansas City Journal*, July 19th., 1881, *Kansas City Star*, July 19th, 1881; *Jesse James, Jr.,* 7-8.

For the remainder of July and all of August, the family lived on Woodland Avenue as the hue and cry subsided. Bill Ryan was brought to Independence to await trial for the Glendale robbery. One would think that Jesse would be any place but there; instead he read in the local papers on July 22nd. an account of his career by his arch enemy, William Pinkerton, and a piece by J.W. Buel, author of *The Border*

Appendix

Outlaws. *Kansas City Journal*, June 14th, July 26th, 1881, *Kansas City Times*, July 22nd, 1881.

At 11 am, August 30th, Jesse and Frank James appeared at the office of H.C. Sailers, a real estate agent, seeking to rent a four-roomed white house on East Ninth Street, a few blocks north of the Woodland address. Evidently Frank was planning to bring his family to Kansas City (they were visiting relatives in California) for they asked to share the house. Sailers refused, saying he did not want "a bedroom turned into a kitchen". They left, but returned at 4 p.m. and agreed to terms. "Jackson" paid a months rent, probably $15.

Kansas City Times, April 6th, 1882.

Clarence and Frank helped him move. Here, they began planning another train robbery. *Trial*, 314; *Kansas City Times*, April 6th, 1881.

Jesse asked Charles Ford to meet them in Independence near the home of Frank's father-in-law on September 6th. They were six: the Jameses and Hites, Ford and Liddle. Their plan to stop an east bound Chicago and Alton Railroad train went awry. There were two trains close together, "and," wrote Clarence, "we did not know which had the most money."

So, they settled down in the woods, and at 9 p.m. on September 7th, stopped the St. Louis Express by piling ties on the tracks and waving a red lantern. No blood was shed this time, in fact, some of the outlaws, Jesse included, seemed "to make sport out of the job," returning money to some passengers and shaking hands with the crew. Jesse gave the engineer $2 "to buy a drink for Jesse James," and introduced himself and Liddle to the engineer, and shouting as he left, "Good-bye, old fellows, this is the last time you will ever see or hear of the James Boys!" In common with the victims of other robberies, some passengers were "inclined to joke and be facetious about the bold robbery."

The gang were on foot (which should have been a clue to the authorities) and walked about half a mile and divided the spoils. After the money was given out, Jesse put the jewelry up for auction, and this money was also divided. Each man received only $140. Jesse kept a nickel-plated stem watch.

Following an old procedure, they divided, some going north; the rest followed the Missouri Pacific tracks through Independence then the C&A into Kansas City and Jesse's house just as a heavy shower began.

Once again they were very daring, very lucky or the authorities very bungling. The train went into Kansas City where a posse boarded a special that ran back to the robbery site, probably passing the outlaws on the way! *Kansas City Times.* September 8th., 1881; *Trial*, 300-310; 315-319.

Jesse, Frank and Clarence Hite stayed in the Ninth Street house for two weeks. Frank James eventually met his family on their return from the west, rented a carriage and boldly drove them to his mother's farm where they remained a few days before taking a train to the east.

Jesse was dissatisfied with the house, described as a "dilapidated old frame concern," especially when it nearly toppled during a severe storm, and rented another at 1017 Troost Avenue, still in the same neighborhood, on October 1st. On November 5th, "something having occurred to arouse the suspicion" of Jesse, they hurriedly moved, loading their possessions on a wagon and with Charles Ford, drove first to Atcheson, Kansas, then St. Joseph, Missouri, arriving on November 9th as "Thomas Howard." He was murdered in this city by Charles and Robert Ford on April 3rd, 1882. *Kansas City Journal*, April 5th, 1882.

What precipitated this hasty flight is not known, but perhaps it was the report in Kansas City papers on October 3lst that he was responsible for killing Ed Miller, a member of his gang, but none of the headlines placed him there, in fact he was said to be in California, Nelson County, Kentucky and embarking for Australia.

Kansas City Star, November 2nd, 1881; *Kansas City Times*, November 3, 4th 1881.

❧

7. The auction was held on April 10th, 1882, only a week after her husband's death. Contrary to expectations, though it attracted an "immense" crowd, bids were very low, not at all what Oscar Wilde, the Irish playwright who visited St. Joseph on April l9th, and others had assumed.

From the World Hotel, in a room with a view of the James home, he wrote an exaggerated account of the sale to illustrate his unfavorable impression of Americans, "Certainly great hero worshippers, and always, take their heroes from the criminal class."

Jesse's coal hod (full of coal) which Wilde claimed had been reserved for a Kansas bidder "at any cost" sold for only $1. The washtub fetched seventy-five cents, not the "income of an English Bishop," and one man whom Wilde wrote had nearly shot another, bought a broom and a scrubbing brush for a quarter.

Top price was paid for young Jesse's little dog which his father had recently given him. Frederick F. Shrader, then a reporter for the *St. Joseph Herald* and later an author and playwright, bought it for $15. The boy's mother gave him the money. *St. Joseph Gazette*, April 11th, 1882; undated newspaper clipping, *James Farm Collection; Cincinnati Enquirer*, April l9th, 1882, *Jesse James, Jr.*, 10.

ใ๛

12. Missouri Pacific train Number 5, from Kansas City to Wichita and Little Rock, was stopped on the east side of Kansas City by a group of men waving a red lantern about 9:40 p.m. on September 23rd, 1898. They detached the engine and express car and moved them about a mile. The safe was blown open, but too much dynamite was used, destroying the car. Only twenty-nine silver dollars were taken.

Jesse James, Jr. was arrested as a participant, October 11th, 1898. Following a trial that attracted national attention because of his name, he was acquitted on February 28th, 1899.

According to her chronology, Stella met young Jesse only a few days before his trial. No wonder her parents were somewhat reluctant for her to see this young man!

She attended each session of his trial. Indeed, a reporter noticed her presence and speculated as to whether she was already Jesse's sweetheart. She was, he said, "one of the most regular attendants ... a sweet faced, dark-eyed girl (who) scarcely took her eyes from the defendant ... When the verdict was read, she staggered ... and kept repeating, "Thank God!""

The next day, Jesse was highly sought after by girls who purchased cigars and pipes just to be able to speak to him. However, Stella gave him a large bouquet of flowers! *Kansas City World*, March 1st, 1899; *New York Herald*, March 4th, 1900.

ใ๛

14. Repeating a family story, Jesse, Jr. claimed the Wisconsin soldier who had shot his father, one "John E. Jones" and Jesse, "became fast friends" and exchanged photo-

graphs. Historians, thus far, have not been able to substantiate the latter part of the story. *Jesse James, Jr.* 57.

ȥ

15. Zee's house was described in 1900 as a "neat little cottage, standing alone on a wide stretch of ground." The interior was sparse, reflecting the family's financial struggles. "In the parlor was a faded Brussels carpet on the floor, an embroidered quotation and pictures of her late husband on the walls, a marble-topped table with a Bible, photo album and several books on it, several chairs and, clean, starched lace curtains at the windows." In addition to the parlor there were two bedrooms and a kitchen. *St. Louis Post Dispatch*, October 8th, 1898; *New York Herald*, March 4th, 1900; *Jesse James, Jr.* 116-117.

ȥ

17. Mary attended school in Kansas City and married Henry L. Barr on March 6th, 1901. They had four children: Lawrence H., Forster Ray, Chester A. and Henrietta who died on October 10th, 1913 at the age of seven months. They lived in a lovely antebellum house opposite the James Farm. It has now been restored by Clay County as the "Claybrook House Historic Site." Mary died on October 11th, 1935.

ȥ

18. Harry Hawley, a musician friend, sang "Without Thee," composed by his accompanist, Charles N. Daniels, for the occasion. About fifty people crowded into the parlor of the row house, part of a court that ran between Broadway and Washington Streets. Among the guests, in addition to those mentioned by Stella, were Frank James and his son

Robert, Mr and Mrs T.T. Crittenden, Jr., R.L. Yeager, E.F. Swinny and Frank P. Wallace, lawyers who defended Jesse Jr. The wedding was front page news in Kansas City and was carried by newspapers all over the nation. Frank James was said to be "almost as happy as his nephew ... and was the life of the party." They spent their honeymoon in the old house on the James Farm.

There were several striking similarities in the weddings of Jesse James, Senior and his son, perhaps intentionally: both were held on the same day of the month: both held in parlors of family homes; the same number of persons were present; Ministers for the Methodist Church, South, performed the ceremony; both brides were Methodists; both were evening affairs; both grooms shared the same famous name and both had been the focus of attention by legal authorities, having been accused of train robbery and both brides had overlooked these allegations; and both couples spent their honeymoons at the James Farm. *Kansas City Journal,* January 25th, l900, *Kansas City Times,* January 25th, 1900.

&

22. Stella, he wrote, "has a slight figure, a girlish, pretty face, and shy manners. She met Jesse before the trial—had 'kept company' with him to some extent—but she did not become seriously interested in him until she saw him at the trial."

The house was cheerful, he said. Zee was very frail and he watched "the slip of a girl busying herself about the house and making everyone happy." *New York Herald,* March 4th, 1900.

Mary James had the responsibility of keeping the keys to a dresser wherein were stored items such as sugar and butter, and refused to give them to Stella until she married and moved away.

(Interview with Ethel Rose Owens, Stella's daughter, April 13th, 1989).

❧

25. His claim of surrendering, questioned by some writers, appears to be verified by a list of guerrilla soldiers who surrendered at Lexington, Missouri, on the dates he mentioned. However, there were fourteen, not forty as published in official correspondence, an error that probably occurred during dictation to a clerk. "J.W. James" was listed as being from Lafayette County and a member of the brigade of Confederate General Jo 0. Shelby—a ruse used by guerrillas to escape retribution by their captors. *Roll of Confederate Soldiers taken the Amnesty Oath, Lexington, Missouri* (War Dept. Collection of Confederate Records, Station Rolls, Missouri) National Archives, Record group 109; *The War of the Rebellion; A Compilation of the Official records of the Union and Confederate Armies* (Washington, D.C. 1880-1902) Series 1, Vol 48, Pt.II 528-529.

❧

26. This is the first publication of a description by Zee of her famous wedding and now permits a more detailed account than has heretofore been possible. Evidently, she and Jesse became serious about each other in 1869, and her parents, who had objected to the relationship because they were first cousins, became "bitterly opposed" to it after Jesse was named an outlaw following the robbery of the bank at Gallatin, Missouri on December 7th 1869 and the murder of the cashier. Of necessity, their courtship had to be conducted in secrecy. He contrived to see her at her parents home in Kansas City, and she, occasionally, stayed with his

mother at the James Farm. On one such evening as they sat in the yard, five men, led by a Pinkerton agent, descended on the house. Not having time to escape, Jesse hid beneath a rose bush, while Zee was secreted "in a fence corner."

Finally, after threatening to elope with Jesse, Zee received the reluctant approval of her mother, (her father had since died). They asked their uncle, Rev. William James, a Methodist minister to perform the ceremony. At first, "Uncle Billy," like her parents, refused, but she insisted. Her reasoning sounded curiously like that of our author, Stella James, a quarter of a century later when she was determined to marry Jesse Junior:She said, reported the minister, "Jesse had been lied about and persecuted, and that he was not half as bad as pictured…. "

They selected April 24th, 1874 as the date and the home of her sister Mrs. W. Boling Browder on South Jefferson Street, Kearney, Missouri, a house that still stands, for the place.

At this time, Jesse was being sought after for Missouri's first train robbery at Gad's Hill, in January that year, and the murder of Pinkerton detective John W. Whicher just a month earlier. Local papers reported he had been seen both in Kansas City and Clay County in mid-April and that the Pinkertons were "working up a case" on him. In fact, on the day of the wedding, the *Liberty Tribune* published a letter from Sheriff George E. Patton, concerning the hunt for the outlaws.

Notwithstanding, Zee rented a carriage from "Colonel" John H. Pemberton, proprietor of the Sheridan Hotel on Fifth Street in Kansas City (probably a family friend as her father had also operated a hotel there) and she and Uncle Billy were driven to Kearney on the morning of the 24th. They left before dawn and may have visited Jesse's mother at the farm.

Jesse bought a new suit of clothes and a pair of boots

for the occasion and, years later, was remembered for riding down the main street of Kearney carrying a Winchester rifle, greeting friends, announcing the wedding. According to one acquaintance, he was invited by Jesse to "Come and see us after we get settled down."

He arrived, he said, late, about 9 p.m., to find about fifty people waiting for him—friends and relatives. Here was his bride to be, "a sweet, modest girl, pretty as a peach ... full of determination" was how one described her. She was, said another, "a most lovely young girl, kind and affectionate and in every way worthy" and still another saw her as "a young lady with an elegant form, beautiful eyes and a face that would be attractive in any assembly." Jesse undoubtedly agreed with them all.

However, Uncle Billy balked and, as he said, "up-braided" Jesse for his reputed deeds. Jesse argued that he was being blamed for more deeds than he could possibly have committed and showed some newspaper clippings from various parts of the country to prove he couldn't have been in those places at the time mentioned. Rev. James relented and performed the ceremony.

The newlyweds visited the old family farm, and this may be why Jesse, Jr. brought Stella here for the same purpose. Mrs. Samuel indicated that Zee stayed in or near Kearney, perhaps with her sister and new mother-in-law, until May 11th when she left by train to join Jesse at the home of Susan James Parmer, his sister, in Sherman, Texas. In June they were in Galveston. Jesse also wrote to several friends that they were going to move to Vera Cruz, Mexico. This was an obvious ploy to mislead the authorities.

In September, they moved to Dallas, then back to Kansas City., using the money he had received from the Gad's Hill robbery to pay for the honeymoon.

Zee never saw her mother again.

"You can say" Jesse instructed a reporter from the *St.*

Louis Dispatch, "that both of us married for love."

    Kansas City Times, April 20th, 1882; *St. Louis Dispatch,* June 9th & October 25th, 1874; *Richmond (Mo) Conservator,* April 11th, 1874; *Kansas City Daily Journal,* April 6th, 1882; *Liberty Tribune,* April 10, 17, 24th, 1874; Robertus Love *The Rise and Fall of Jesse James,* (St. Louis, 1926) 277.

ᔑ

    30. Zee died of "sciatic rheumatism and nervous prostration" at 5:25 am. She had been confined to bed for eleven months and lapsed into unconsciousness on November 9th. *Kansas City Journal,* November 15th, 1900.

    "It was a simple yet impressive ceremony yesterday afternoon when the body of Mrs. Zerelda James … was taken from the little home at 3402 Tracy Avenue, and placed in a receiving vault at Elmwood Cemetery. The home which she loved so well and in which her children had grown up was filled with relatives and friends and many floral emblems had been contributed which were used to decorate the small parlor where the casket lay. A dozen or more old neighbors from Clay County were there and Frank James…had come from St Louis … Some of Kansas City's eldest citizens were there to pay their last respects to the memory of a good woman universally loved and respected.

    "When the rooms had been filled so that not another person could gain admittance, a sweet, tender voice began a song. It was "What a Friend we Have in Jesus" (the same hymn sung at Jesse's funeral on April 6th, 1882). After this … Rev. M. B. Chapman … spoke feelingly of the character of the woman who, by her Christian example, had won the most tender affection of all who knew her…. 'In all of the trials which filled her tempestuous life, she never did an unworthy act ….'" *Ibid,* November 14th, 1900.

    Jesse, Jr. testified that she left very little money, "wholly insufficient to pay her debts," so he sold the house for $1,300 on April 1st, 1901 to pay the bills. When the estate was settled, he received only $293.00 and Mary $75.00. Jackson County, Mo. Probate Records A+16-P-206.

᠔

32. Frank James chose the pallbearers, and he and young Jesse invited them from Kearney, June 23rd, 1902. Frank James to Warren Welch, June 23rd, 1902 asking him to be present when they would "remove from the old farm the remains of Brother Jesse and renter it *(sic)* at this place." Jesse E. James to same: asking for six of Jesse's "war companions to act as Pall Bearers *(sic)*." Warren Welch Papers, Jackson County Historical Society Archives, Independence, Mo.

᠔

34. Robert and Charles Ford, the gang members who killed Jesse James, testified at the inquest after his murder that they and Jesse arrived at the James Farm on Thursday evening March 23rd., 1882, intending to stay with his mother. However, "friends of the family ... Jesse had no wish to see" were visiting John Samuel, who had been severely wounded in a shooting incident, so they hid in the barn until they left. The group stayed at the house all of Friday, then visited the Nicholsons, staying in the barn before going to St. Joseph, Saturday. On the way, they stopped at a church 18 miles from the city during a rainstorm. *St. Joseph Gazette* April 5th, 1882.

39. On September 30th, 1852, Zerelda Cole James married Benjamin A. Simms, a wealthy widower, twenty-five years her senior, creating a controversy in her family and a puzzle for historians. Why did she marry a man nearly twice her age? Why did the marriage fail? How did she and Simms meet and where did they live?

He was from an old and distinguished family. His father, Richard Simms, Jr. was a Revolutionary War veteran, having fought on Long Island, at Brandywine and Stony Point, and suffered the misery of Valley Forge with the 3rd Virginia Regiment. After the war he married and sired ten children. Benjamin, born about 1800, was the eighth. He served with the Virginia Militia in 1814 during the War of 1812, and moved with his father to Kentucky, and then to Clay County, Missouri. He had a farm near his father's and three hundred and eighty acres in Clinton County.

How he met and courted the vivacious young widow James is not known, but Robert S. James had been as well known as any man in the county and had founded Providence Baptist Church near Simms' farm. The death of Robert was reported in the same issue of the *Liberty Tribune* as that of Richard Simms. (October 25th, 1850) Though Simms has been called a "neighbor" their farms were more than seven miles apart.

It was, by all accounts, an unhappy marriage. "The lady alleges," wrote the anonymous author of a Clay County history published in 1885, "that the chief trouble arose from the fact that her three little children, Frank, Jesse and Susie, whom she had always humored and indulged, gave their old stepfather no end of annoyance." Simms had raised one family and had been "a strict disciplinarian." At his insistence, she agreed to send them away to relatives but her "near relatives" threatened to ostracize her, so she relented.

Her bitterness caused her to withdraw from the New Hope Church. She maintained that Simms "always treated her with kindness."

Notwithstanding, it is evident she did place the children in the care of someone for she moved to his home in northern Clinton County and probably suffered a miscarriage there. Probate records of Simms' estate in Clinton County contain nineteen notations by Dr. Absolam Kerns, who attended the lady from January 9th to March 15th, 1853. A crisis occurred on March 8th when Dr. Kerns "gave her medicine and close attention all day and night and next day until the p.m." He stayed two more nights.

She returned to her home in the spring and the tradition is that she planned a divorce before his death on January 2nd, 1854. *The Simms Family of Stafford County, Virginia*, 11-18; 40-42; Anon. *History of Clay and Platte Counties* (St. Louis, 1885) 266; *Kansas City Times,* Feb. 13th, 1911; *Liberty Tribune*, Jan 6th, 1854.

An interesting by-product of this marriage was that Frances Peters Inskeep, a niece of Simms, married Coleman Purcell Younger of Clay County on March 17th, 1852 and moved to San Jose, California. A nephew named for this Younger, was the outlaw, Cole Younger.

Mary, the younger sister of Frances, married Martin Ringo on September 5th, 1848 and also went to San Jose. Their son, John Peters was the "Johnny Ringo" of Tombstone, Arizona fame. Zerelda was therefore, by marriage the great aunt of the Youngers and Ringo, and her sons, cousins, but only by marriage, not blood. *Simms Family*, 64-65.

Also a product of this strange marriage was another very distant relationship. Adaline Younger, who married James Lewis Dalton in 1851 and became the mother of Bob, Grat and Emmett, the core of the famous Dalton Gang, was the half-sister of Coleman Purcell Younger. In effect, this made the James Boys, the Youngers, Ringo and the Daltons distant cousins.

A further coincidence is revealed by the recent discovery that Bruce Younger, half-brother of Coleman, married Maybelle Reed (better known as Belle Star) in Chetopa, Kansas, on May 15th, 1880. Though this marriage was brief, it succeeded in bringing the name of another famous outlaw into this curious relationship. Marley Brant, "Bruce Younger, The Man, the Myth and the Mummy." *True West*, Vol 36 #3 (March, 1989) 38-39.

ॐ

40. To historians, Dr. Reuben Samuel has been a shadowy, pitiful figure; present during most of the James saga, yet vague and distant, so vague his biography has never been written. A stepfather of the James boys, he was much loved and was affectionately called "Pappy." His aim had been to send the children to college, instead he became a victim of the times.

He was born in Owen County, Kentucky on January 12th, 1828, son of Fielding Samuel and was named for a grandfather. He first came to Clay County in 1840 with his father, then attended the Medical College of Ohio in Cincinnati, 1850-51. He began practicing in Liberty in 1854, then Greenville, a village three miles east of the James Farm. His office was in the store of William James, the brother-in-law of Zerelda. Their families surely knew one another as the farms were less than a mile apart, and she often stopped at the James store. By all accounts Zerelda was "very good looking and lively" when they married on September 12th, 1855. Dr. Samuel was "a bit bashful" and instead of confronting her he slipped "billet dous" in her sewing basket where they would sometimes remain days or weeks before she found them.

Dr. Samuel was hanged several times by Federal militia during a raid on the farm on May 25th, 1863. Frank James was by then with a Confederate guerrilla unit that had just taken Plattburg, Missouri, county seat of Clinton County and had been tracked in that direction. The rope evidently hampered the flow of blood to his brain, and though he survived, he was "not ... right in his mind" afterwards. *Liberty Tribune*, December 15th, 1893; *Medical College of Ohio, Annual Announcement of Lectures...and Catalog of Students and Graduates* (Cincinnati, Ohio, 1857); *James Farm Journal II, #1,* (March 1984) ; Philip W. Steele. *Jesse and Frank James the Family History* (Gretna, La. 1989) 63-66.

&

42. A typical tour was reported as follows:

"A correspondent...visited the home of... (the) mother of the James boys .... The Samuel Farm is one of the best in the county. On arriving ... Mrs. Samuel opened (the door) and kindly invited us in.

She is a large, portly woman, close on to six feet tall, very graceful and easy-bearing.

She talked of Jesse and Frank, as to how they lived and the many means ... employed ... to effect their capture.

Mrs. Samuel spoke of many unkind things that had been said to her; of how her true character had been misrepresented by the world. She said:

"I know that the James boys have done wrong...but they were driven to it ... then outlawed and not permitted to settle down and live the lives of ordinary citizens. Jesse wrote three Governors (of Missouri) asking (to) surrender ... He never received any reply. ... I think since Frank's surrender his conduct and citizenship have been such as to win approval and respect."

As she took her visitors on a tour of the home she re-marked, "I remember well, when I was the age of you young people, how my beaux used to come see me. Oh what happy days then; but, alas, what sad days I have experienced since that halcyon period! The trouble and anxiety I have suffered! Two boys out in the world, liable at any time to meet with a tragic death! Could I … forsake them?" *Darlington* (Wisconsin) *Republican*; June 10th, 1889.

❧

44. Mary Ellen Hill, a 17-year-old Kentucky girl, was Mrs. Samuel's maid for six months in 1909. According to Mary, she was cantankerous, fiesty and had a black humor. She played practical jokes in the same style as described by Stella. For example she would toss the casing of the explosive that had been thrown in the cabin at Mary on the porch, to scare her. Mrs. Samuel did little housework and was a poor cook.

"She called herself a white elephant," Mary recalled, and often sang,"I'm wild and wooly and hard to tame; My name is Zerelda just the same." Oral History Interview with Mary Ellen Clemmons, October 13th, 1979; James Collection.

❧

50. "Mrs. Zerelda Samuels *(sic)* … died in the Pullman car of a St. Louis & San Francisco passenger train twenty miles from Oklahoma City at 3 o'clock this afternoon. (She) had spent two months visiting her son, Frank James,…near Fletcher, Ok. She and her daughter-in-law, Mrs. Frank James, were on their way to Kansas City to visit Mrs. Samuel's grandson, Jesse James, Jr." *Kansas City Times,* February 11th, 1911.

ॐ

54. When visitors came to the James Farm for tours by Robert James or his wife, Annie James would retreat into the South Parlor and close the door. She never gave an interview about her life with Frank. She would visit only with family or close friends. Yet, hers was the most exciting and romantic courtship and wedding of them all. It is the stuff that great novels, plays and movies are made of; but it was hers and she never shared it.

Anna ("Annie") Ralston was born on January 25th, 1853 on her father's farm outside Independence, Missouri. Her father, Samuel Ralston, was a prominent citizen in the community who lost much of his property as a result of the Civil War. Though he was a strong supporter of the South, the Irish-born Ralston did not serve in the army. However, his home was a rendezvous for various groups of Confederates, (including Frank James) which caused him to be removed as a result of Order Number 11, a Union measure to depopulate the rebel-supporting countryside.

Anna graduated from the Independence Female College on June 21st, 1872 with a B.A. degree in Science and Literature. She became a schoolteacher. She was described as a "gay, laughter-loving member of the society of Independence ... the apple of her father's eye." She went to dances, fishing and boating parties, picnics, but most of all, she was a "magnificent" horsewoman and a "superb" pistol shot. She was "about the best rider in the county...She used a side saddle and her slim body seemed almost part of the spirited mount.... More than one man felt heart tremors when he saw her. But to none of them did ... (she) ever give more than a passing smile and wave of her slender hand." Paul I Wellman, "The Girl who eloped with Frank James," *Kansas City Star,* July 16th, 1944.

Except for Frank James. How they began their courtship is unknown. One family story has it that it occurred during a croquet party when they renewed their wartime acquaintance, except this time they fell in love. Frank returned several times. Evidently, when she took a job as teacher of the school at Little Santa Fe, Missouri, an old trail village south of Kansas City, they were able to carry on a romance. "The idea that he wanted my daughter for his wife or that she would accept him never entered my head," said her father.

One day in June, 1874, she told her father she wanted to visit her brother-in-law, Ezra Hickman, in Kansas City and a former schoolmate in Omaha. Ralston took her to the Chicago & Alton Depot in Independence where she took the train. (Ironically the same railroad her future husband would rob nearby). On the way to Kansas City, she sat with a family friend, who thought she seemed "rather excited." Hickman was there to greet her but she claimed the need to speak to a friend still on the train and suggested that he go home and she would take the hack. That was the last seen of her.

A few days later her mother received a letter:"Dear Mother. I am married and going West *(sic)*. Annie Reynolds."

Stunned, Ralston and his sons tried to trace and find "Reynolds" whom they feared was a gambler, but to no avail. Later that year, her brother, John, saw T.M. James, uncle of Frank, at his china importing business in Kansas City. When introduced, James smiled. I am glad to meet you," he said. "My nephew, Frank James, has married your sister."

"Astounded" the younger man went home and broke the news to a shocked Sam Ralston.

He disowned her.

She and Frank had apparently gone to Omaha to be married and then joined Jesse, Zee and Susie in Texas.

Two years later Frank got up enough nerve to pay a visit to his father-in-law. It was not a pleasant occasion.

"He arrived early in the morning," related Ralston, "but refused...to get off his horse...but at last did...and took breakfast with us, but did not take the saddle from his horse...He talked about Annie a good deal and said she was well, and wanted to know if 'I had forgiven him'. I told him he was a dammed rascal and had stolen my daughter and I wanted her to come back. He stated that if I did not forgive her she would not return and in any case I would not see her for ten years. I replied that his life was so uncertain that his wife ought to be free in a place of safety, but he only said, 'By God, she shan't come back and you shan't see her,' and then mounted his horse and rode away."

Imagine! Frank James, the most sought after outlaw in the country, afraid to dismount and face his father-in-law! *Kansas City Times, Ibid*; Croy, *Jesse James was my Neighbor*, 218-223.

She shared the existence of an outlaw, living under aliases in Texas, Tennessee, Maryland, Virginia, in small, unpretentious houses. Though Ralston claimed he never saw her for eight years, there is evidence that indicates he relented and she visited him several times. In the summer of 1882, she, and Zerelda Samuel, interceded to arrange for Frank's surrender to Governor T.T. Crittenden of Missouri, on October 5th of that year. There are long love letters Frank wrote from jails in Independence and Gallatin in Missouri and Huntsville, Alabama, awaiting his trials, revealing the enormous stress she was under. She appeared at both trials, lovely, ladylike and noble, and shared their long life after his acquittals, when he was working as a shoe clerk, theatre doorman, race starter and farmer. When he died at the Farm on January 18th, 1915, her only comment was: "A better husband never lived."

Why a talented, beautiful, well-raised girl like her

would marry an outlaw has long intrigued historians. She was twenty-one, he thirty-one. He courted her openly— she, like Zee and Stella, with their men, also knew who he was.

Once, in Kansas City while walking down a street they chanced on a policeman trying to restrain a drunk. Spotting Frank, he asked him for help. Thinking quickly, Frank used the excuse he needed to catch a train, and paid another to serve in his stead.

But Frank liked literature (her college major). He read and recited Shakespeare. They went to the theatre in all the large cities, especially New York. She seemed happy and never appeared to have regretted her decision.

She continued to live at the old Farm with her son and his wife. She loved to read and sew but gradually lost her sight.

She died on July 6th, 1944 and her ashes are buried beside Frank's in Hill Cemetery, Independence, Missouri.

Every one remembers "Aunt Anna" as a perfect lady.

ও

60. "At 9th and Main and Delaware just north of the C & A office was the Soda Fountain and Candy Shop *(sic)* of Jesse James, Jr.," he wrote. "I was a pupil at Spaldings *(sic)* Commercial College in the New York Life Bldg. *(sic)* in 1901 and early 1902, studying debit and credit and Pittman Shorthand. Carfare and a quarter for lunch was all I received when I left home—

"Well, on one occasion *(sic)* I stopped in Jesse's place and had an Ice cream Soda *(sic)*—5 cents. When I'd finished it—I found I had no nickel only a car ticket home. Jesse said, 'Oh, that's all right, pay when you come again.' I paid the next day! My father stood for honesty." *Kansas City Star*, September 4th, 1980.

In 1964, Stella James visited former President Truman in his office at the Harry S. Truman Library, Independence, Missouri, where they reminisced about those days. *Independence Examiner*, July 17th, 1964.

᠈᠘

62. He became known as a good "book" lawyer, and associates said he never lost a case in appellate court because of an improperly prepared petition. He was quoted as saying, "I shall never specialize in criminal practice. There isn't enough money in that…work…the money is in corporation law and in will cases." *Kansas City Star*, March 27th, 1951; *Kansas City Law Journal* (June 7th, 1906) *Pendex* (Student Body, Kansas City School of Law, 1907).

᠈᠘

65. Jesse, Jr., his friend Harry C. Hoffman and Franklin B. Coates, a film writer and director from New York were originally signed by "Mecca Pictures" to make the movie. However, friction developed and the three withdrew and signed with Mesco.

The officers and directors of Mesco Pictures Corporation were Kansas Citians. Jesse's good friend Thomas T. Crittenden was Vice President and Hoffman (who played Cole Younger, even though an article early on said he was going to be sheriff) General Manager. According to the prospectus Mesco was organized "to produce only the best photoplays possible." Its capital was $250,000, divided into 2,500 shares of common stock at a par value of $100.

The prospectus included a letter written by Jesse, Jr. on August 2nd 1920, in which he makes the incredible claim that Coates' script was "authentic in every respect."

Jesse signed two contracts:one, on August 14th, 1920

was for him to be paid $50,000 for starring in the film. "No scene…shall portray Jesse James in the perpetuation *(sic)* of any train or bank robbery … " The second, dated August 15th, 1921 was for personal appearances with the film outside of Missouri at a rate of $25 a day, plus expenses. A voucher found with the contracts indicates he received a total of only $32,400.

Stock was sold to friends and relatives.

The movie was filmed at various sites around Kansas City. Jesse played both himself and his father and Stella played herself. Other actors besides Hoffman and Coates were Diana Reed and Margurete Hungerford. It purported to show Jesse, Jr. in 1920 discussing with Coates a book the latter had written about Jesse James' Civil War experiences. Suddenly (by a great coincidence) the airplane of a millionaire sportsman flying from coast to coast is forced down next to Jesse, Jr.'s house. The pilot meets Lucille, Jesse's beautiful eldest daughter and it was love at first sight. As the romance builds, Jesse, Jr. gives the beau a copy of the book which explains the history of the girl's family. Then the picture was a series of flashbacks to the Civil War.

It was promoted as "an authentic, spectacular, gigantic portrayal of … Jesse James. A photoplay that Should Gain a Half Million Dollars or More" *(sic)*.

The film opened at theatres in early 1921 and was advertised as a "A historically true romance of incidents that are part of the legend of Missouri." Jesse, Jr. was away making personal appearances much of the time. However, it was a critical as well as a financial failure. According to his daughter Ethel Rose Owens, he used all the money he received to pay back as many investors as possible, leaving himself in such a precarious position that he had to sell his house. *James Farm Collection*; for contracts & prospectus; *Kansas City Star*, July 25th, August 1st, 1920; March 15th, 1921; Oral History interview with Ethel Rose Owens. April

13th, 1989. *James Farm Collection.*

Actually, *Jesse James Under the Black Flag* was "Book 1" of two films, the second was called *Jesse James the Outlaw.* After years of searching, the editor learned in 1989 of a print that was stored in a barn in Northern California. It is a combination of both films and is in such good condition that video cassettes have been made of it.

❧

67. Excelsior Springs, Missouri, April 16th (1932)—The man who has lived here several months as the famous outlaw, Jesse James, was repudiated this afternoon by Mrs. Jesse James, Jr., after a public hearing. Sixteen of the eighteen "old timers" at the gathering denounced his claims.

The group had gathered in a room at the Royal Hotel to hear his answers to questions the real Jesse ... would have been able to answer. Mrs. Jesse James, Jr., had come all the way from Los Angeles to investigate the claims on behalf of her husband who is in ill health.

As questions were asked and old events recalled, the fiery emotions of another day were stirred ... the boots, the spurs and the guns of the outlaw laid on a table before them were little less than sacred.

The denouncement came with the questioning of Frank Milburn who made the boots that Jesse James wore at his wedding and who took Mrs. Samuel, the mother...to St. Joseph when James was killed.

"No, he isn't Jesse James," Mr. Milburn said, and pointing to Perry Samuel ... "not any more than that ... Fellow...."

"Why Jesse James wore 6½ shoes. ... This fellow couldn't get those boots on."

The boots ... were held up ... they were two inches too short.

"Those weren't my boots," the claimant had said, "those aren't my spurs nor is any of that stuff mine."

"Then why did my husband's mother value them so?" Mrs. James asked."If they were fakes, she had plenty of chances to sell them. But she made me swear I would never part with them."

"Mrs. James ... questioned the old man kindly ... 'I have not come to hurt anyone,' the dark eyed little woman ... said... 'I have grown to like this old man ... but I want the truth established.'" *Kansas City Star*, April 17th, 1932.

The boots, spurs, guns and other effects were presented to the James Farm Museum by the family of Jesse James, Jr. on August 5th, 1988.

ॐ

68. The old man making the claim was one "J. Frank Dalton," who claimed, among other things that he had lived in Brazil, been a lawyer, and a pilot in World War I.

Dalton was taken under the wing of the operator of a Missouri cave (who once tried to climb the Empire State Building in an tiger suit) and allowed him to claim that (as Jesse) he had used the cave as a hideout.

In 1950, Dalton petitioned a Missouri court to change his name to Jesse James. This was denied, the judge saying, "If he is what he professes to be he is trying to perpetuate a fraud upon this Court. If he is Jesse James ... then my suggestion would be that he retreat to his rendezvous and ask the good God above to forgive him.... "

Undaunted, a promoter announced on national television February 27th, 1967, that he would pay $10,000 to anyone who could prove him wrong on his insistence that Dalton was the real James. Stella and her daughters Ethel Rose Owens and Estelle Baumel challenged him. When he refused to pay they sued him. The trial was held in Union,

Missouri on May 6th, 1970. The jury agreed with Stella. However, the promoter appealed and on June 14th, 1972, the St.
Louis Court of Appeals unanimously upheld the verdict.
Dalton died alone in Grandberry, Texas on August 15th,
1951.

The promoter conveniently overlooked the trial verdict in his publications about his "Jesse James." Steve Eng,
"The Great Outlaw Hoax," *True West*, XXXIII #2 (February,
1986;) 17-23.

69. Howk made the assertion that Jesse James and his
comrades had been part of a nebulous underground organization known as "The Knights of the Golden Circle"
dedicated to starting a second Civil War, and had guns and
fabulous amounts of money hidden in caves under certain
cities. None has ever been recovered. Howk died on July
26th, 1984 Eng, *Ibid.*

70. *Bitter Harvest* was a made-for-TV film shown on
the CBS series "Playhouse 90" and starred Franchot Tone as
Frank James and James Drury as Jesse, Jr. "The two ... come
back to their...home town hoping to live peaceably ... but
the town's brass won't have it, and a bank robbery, a fight
and a chase following ... make things difficult."

Stella tried to prevent its showing in court. "I understand that the right to privacy is the right to be left alone," her
grandson James Ross argued." We saw the show and it is not
true or even partly true. Does a man lose his right to privacy
just because he has that name?"

"If you're Jesse James, you are in the public eye," the
judge ruled, denying the petition. *Los Angeles Times*, April
17th, 1958; *Kansas City Star*, April 17th, 1958.

The James Farm National Historic Site

Jesse W. James, the world famous outlaw, was born in the log house that still stands at the James Farm Historic Site, near Kearney, Missouri, September 5, 1847. The farm had been purchased by the Rev. Robert S. James, a Baptist minister, and his wife, Zerelda, in 1845, after they moved to Missouri from Kentucky. They had one child at that time, Alexander Franklin, born in 1843. A sister, Susan, was born after Jesse.

The log house was built in 1822 and is one of the oldest structures between western Missouri and California. An Eastlake cottage was added to the log cabin by their mother in 1893. All of the furnishings are original and were acquired with the house when it was purchased with 40 acres of the original farm, from three of the grandsons of Jesse James by the Clay County Department of Parks, Recreation and Historic Sites, and is open daily for tours.

The James Farm Museum was built in 1987 and houses collections of artifacts that belonged to Jesse and Frank

James and other members of the family and their outlaw confederates. The exhibits and an audio-visual presentation tell the story. An outdoor historical drama, *The Life and Times of Jesse James,* is professionally produced and acted at the Site each August. Nearby is Claybrook House, a beautifully restored antebellum house that was the home of Mary James Barr, only daughter of Jesse James.

Jesse James, his wife and other members of his family are buried in Mt. Olivet Cemetery in nearby Kearney, Missouri.

The site is adjacent to I-35, 20 miles north of Kansas City, Missouri.

———————◆———————

A product of

The Revolver Press
A Division of Dragon Books
P.O. Box 6039. Thousand Oaks,
CA 91359 USA